# COLLECT
# VALUE
# DIVEST

ELIZABETH STEWART Ph.D.

Certified Member, AAA, Appraisers Association of America

Author services by Kathleen Kaiser & Associates.
www.KathleenKaiserAndAssociates.com

Publishing services by Pedernales Publishing, LLC.
www.pedernalespublishing.com

Book Interior and Cover design:
Mary Schlesinger, Schlesinger Design
www.schlesingerdesign.com

Author photo: John Flandrick

Library of Congress Control Number: 2016954479

ISBN 978-0-9981025-0-4 Paperback Edition
ISBN 978-0-9981025-2-8 Digital Edition

Printed in the United States of America

To Shawn Lozeau,

Irreplaceable

and

John Flandrick,

Invaluable

# CONTENTS

I BELIEVE YOU HOLD A VALUABLE BOOK
in your hands, dear collector. These are my top secret files that will
forever change your relationship to *objets d'art*. These are case studies of
collectors with whom I've worked for the past 30 years as a professional
certified appraiser and whom I've helped to discover great value. You'll
find that a good many antiques, collectibles, and pieces of art harbor an amazing historical life, and reflect significantly upon each of
their owners.

Using real-life situations, I discuss how an expert goes about appraising
art, and you will learn these techniques for yourself. I also discuss frauds,
fakes, forgeries, and damaged and stolen works in specific and lively detail.
Each chapter recounts a work of art entering or exiting a collector's life. By
"entering," I mean how the object was acquired, and, by "exiting," how it was

sold, lost, stolen, or given away. I also instruct on material, form, composition, and history in formulating a theory of value.

In the first chapter, you'll realize just how important your nose is, along with other senses, in judging authenticity. In the very first case study, my client claimed to have inherited an F. Remington painting. If it "smelled" right, this most fortunate client had actually inherited a cool SIX MILLION! By the time you finish this book you'll be able to sniff out value.

These case studies track many of the challenges you'll meet in a fluid market, which has reached a new tipping point with so many Boomers. You'll find a section on this recent wave in the "Nostalgia" chapter.

You'll also find valuations in trending categories, such as mid-century dolls, old cast-iron toys, old board games, TVs, old record players, LP vinyl records, real vintage apparel, and Christmas items. To those many collectors who fondly remember the era from whence these object hail, these

items are worth gold. Also included is a section on books, highlighting two amazing discoveries springing from my own office. First, a text from the era of the Knights Templar and next the appearance of another rare text: that of an irreplaceable Nazi-confiscated 9th-century religious piece, appraised for millions.

I point out how provenance (from whence an item stems) contributes to its value specifically with jewelry, metal, and stone antiquities.

You will laugh about the curious specimens sought by certain collectors, such as Galileo's fingers or an actual vial of President Reagan's dried blood. And along with those are stories of "the one that got away."

I offer data on what's currently hot as well as the buzz on top investments for the upcoming marketplace. You'll find step-by-step instruction on best-practice strategies for building a robust collection. I even venture into the realm of extreme collecting, also known as hoarding, in response to a collector asking: "Am I a hoarder?"

You'll find the most vital how-tos: how to buy, sell, downsize, insure, invest, and attend auctions. I also offer important advice on how to bequeath, parcel out, and include your items in estate plans—and why you should care now. These are valuable nuggets culled from decades of consultations on client collections and their divestiture. Getting rid of stuff is an ongoing dilemma and I address the thorny issue of whether to sell (what's the best venue for the most profit) or to donate.

*Collect, Value, Divest* aptly describes the process of collecting and assessing value in a fluid market, and it's more critical than ever to seek out expert advice. How does one go about establishing true authentication, targeting the best online resources, avoiding swindles, and dealing with sentimental factors?

Today, it's essential to be astute and skilled — to know your stuff.

When I began appraising almost 30 years ago, there were no shows on appraising, selling, picking, or buying art and antiques. Today that information is highly prized, as evidenced by the over 30 TV channels airing weekly sub-genre reality shows on hunting for stuff. The two most popular, *Antiques Roadshow* and *Pawn Stars*, reveal mountains about our current relationship to the material world.

Years ago I was employed as a research assistant for an *Antiques Roadshow*-style event, and I will now debunk a few myths for a real insider's peek. Shows like *Antiques Roadshow* look quite spontaneous but they are not. Perhaps the long line of people holding stuff is the reality, but pickers will only motion to the good stuff and wave those over to an appropriate appraiser. Many others are loaded with pure junk: one claimed she had a real antique clock from her great-great-great-grandmother. But after a cursory look, I realized it had a nice long electric cord!

Appraisers at such events assess items and research them with plenty of advance time. Instead of staying and waiting to hear about their items on the spot, owners may wait and sometime later, those with interesting items get a call to come on.

If the item is still right for the show, the owners may be cosmetically made up for the camera and instructed on acting surprised.

They appear as though they've just

simply been pulled out of line and informed on the spot of what actually was gleaned from years of research.

Of course, this is not reality, but neither is reality TV. How about *Storage Wars*, which features many badly dressed people with way too much time on their hands? With a mere glance at mounds of stuff, these buyers immediately jump into the auction. They make offers on abandoned storage lockers without entering to investigate the contents. After the purchase, a few claim to have made it big to justify staggeringly high prices paid for junk. Yet it takes years to become savvy enough to uncover a needle in a haystack, just as it takes years to develop that sixth sense about a collector from seeing only a few of their items. The chances of an uneducated person getting lucky with a huge find are practically nil. And most stuff in the average locker is hideous.

Then there is *American Pickers*, the oddest show I've ever seen. The two pickers are a couple of cool,

jive guys replete with facial hair and tattoos and the switchboard gal is a hip, no-bull dispatcher. If you haven't seen the show, "Rosie" directs these guys to hick towns in search of any barn, garage, or attic treasures. Sans Rosie, I've done the same, but getting good footage out of cockroach-infested barns is challenging (let alone to discover the valuable items). I propose the sole reason anyone calls these guys to purchase their stuff is that they hope to be on air.

*Hoarders* is perhaps the worst

of all collecting reality shows, and it curdles my blood. Hoarding can often be life-threatening, a pathology. I know this from having experienced 23 hoarders in my 30 years of appraising. Sadly, all 23 are now dead. Hoarding is likely to have been the cause of death, whether from infections due to filth and vermin, the eventual collapse of piled-up walls, or house fires.

What a terrible way to die! Yet this exploitative show sensationalizes the disorder. We would not torture someone suffering from a sad and possibly fatal mental disorder, so why persecute hoarders on air?

The only reason I force myself to watch is to add to my research on public opinion and the world of material culture. We've become obsessed with stuff and now have so much that our possessions no longer contribute to a beautiful or useful

life. These commodities constantly demand more of our time and money but as we amass more stuff, it feeds the obsession.

I close my defense of writing a book about Stuff for the Collector in you with an eye-popping list of shows: *Storage Wars, Antiques UK, American Treasures, Auction Kings, Oddities, Buried Treasure, Cash and Cari, Cash in the Attic, American Pickers, Canadian Pickers, Accidental Fortune, American Restoration, Pawn Stars, Picker Sisters, Auction Packed, It's Worth What?, History Detective, Auction Hunters, Hollywood Treasure, Hoarders, Auctioneer$, My Collection Obsession, Hardcore Pawn, Cajun Pawn Stars, Comic Book Men, Combat Cash* (wartime collectibles), *All Star Dealers* (sports collectibles), *Ball Boys* (also sports), *The Great Big American Auction,* and *Antique Warriors.*

Each of these will waste a perfectly good hour of your time. And none will instruct on the methodology of digging for gold in a trove of Stuff. That is what this book offers: a motherlode of nuggets based on real-life experiences. You'll find all the precious tools of a seasoned appraiser at the top of her game.

## A REMINGTON? SEE & SMELL IT FIRST:

# CAUGHT

I KNEW THERE WOULD BE TROUBLE when I researched the last auction sale of a Remington: one of his paintings just sold for $5.6 million. My client unveiled that he had inherited a painting signed by Frederic Remington, and indeed it looked much like Remington's *Caught in the Circle* presently in Fort Worth's Sid Richardson Museum. Remington was prolific in the first quarter of the 20th century and my client had what appeared to be a copy of this image on older canvas. Or maybe *not* a copy at all (he hoped). Sadly, in the final analysis, this case study will show you *how we discovered the painting was an unauthorized (though honest and excellent) student copy.*

You might know that some artists paint their most popular image(s) more than once, and some reproduce these in authorized prints. Depending upon how popular they are (how many of those prints are in the market), the prints may simply be copied as master works by art students. And some students who are more talented than wise might also *sign* the artist's name.

To ascertain whether my client had an actual reproduction painting or an artist's reproduced painting, I would either have to be an expert in Remington's brush strokes (I am not) or I would have to employ deductive skills based on the most likely best- and worst-case scenarios, given the artist's popularity.

I needed to figure out just how popular the image was. If it was admired, the likelihood that it was a copy was greater, but if it was *not* a copy, we'd have $5.6 million at stake. This case study demonstrates the tried and true appraisers' approach to research: *the belief that the object you hold is absolutely original and valuable.* Start by believing in the best-case scenario, comparing what you have to the *best* comparables out there, and then sift the results as you deduce down from Authentic to Copy (not the other way around). If you're sure you are a gold digger like me, remember: if it's too good to be true, it just *might* be true. Or prove it otherwise. I researched exactly how many of Remington's popular works were

early 20th century those deceptive reproduction techniques were just developing, so I needed to excavate unauthorized reproductions in the comparable marketplace. Depending on just how many were out there, the likelihood of a copy could increase.

I started with an overview of his authorized images rendered in the most affordable medium—prints on paper—starting with the first issues done during his lifetime. Keep in mind, I was preparing for the second part of the process, which would be to draft a letter of my findings to a museum known for Remingtons and to send on photos. Remember, too, we can't ask a museum to quote value; they can only help authenticate.

Chromolithography is a type of color lithograph and an early process of reproduction. Remington was famous for publishing portfolios of images he'd either drawn or painted previously, using this print medium. An example is the oil painting *Antelope Hunting,* converted by Remington's studio into a chromolithograph in his lifetime. In 2016, it was offered for sale by the Philadelphia Print Shop. This single print from the Remington portfolio was published in 1889 in Boston by Whidden Publishing Company as

reproduced in authorized versions over the years. I got acquainted with the artist's work. I also examined his medium of reproduction—and this step is crucial. *Medium* refers to the material or substance the artist uses to create their artwork; for instance, duplicated oil on canvas, oil pastel on paper, or various print on paper techniques. I needed to uncover how many famous images (and multiple versions of those) existed by this artist.

My knowledge of print and painting techniques proved indispensable. I knew that both print and painting reproductions occurred early in the 20th century when Remington was alive. As new computer technologies developed, *more* prints were reproduced as authorized prints. In the part of the artist's authorized collection and the set was entitled *Sport, or Shooting and Fishing.* The asking price today is $1,250 for the original 1889 print edition.

Note that if an authorized version contemporaneous with the artist's life is currently selling for $1,250, we can deduce that the original chromolithograph was likely not that expensive and that there are many out there, which keeps pricing more affordable than the rarer paintings. If a painting by this artist can sell for $5.6 million, the rarity factor is important to valuation.

Another noteworthy Remington reproduction is a portfolio entitled *A Bunch of Buckskins*, a set of chromolithographs published by R.H. Russell in 1901. These eight images were and are often separated from the intact, whole portfolio and are sold as separate prints. The series *A Bunch of Buckskins* was originally created by Remington in oil pastel, which his printer then reproduced as chromolithographs. So here we have both works of the same image in two mediums and both authorized by the artist. Some of the titles in this portfolio are among the most sought after of his prints: *An Old Time Trapper, An Arizona Cowboy, A Blackfoot Brave,* and *A Northwest Half Breed.*

These chromolithographs are not at all small, with some as large as 20 by 15 inches and they sell today for around $2,000 each, an indication that Remington prints were found in the medium-range market of the first quarter of the 20th century.

Armed with all the above clues, we can make an assumption: any art student wishing to copy a Remington would have had access to a plethora of fairly inexpensive images had they tried to "match" the master. Art students were (and are) notoriously poor, however, so could there be cheaper early 20th-century copies of *Caught*?

Collier & Sons of New York had published very affordable Remington halftone prints back in the day. Under a magnifying glass, halftones appear to be dots (like newsprint) and they vary: gray variations for black-and-white prints and color dots for colored prints. In the halftone portfolio authorized by Remington entitled *Done in the Open* from 1903, the halftone prints are not as valuable as the chromolithographs we researched earlier: today an 8-by-12-inch print sells for only $150. Now we come to the biggest piece of my client's oil painting puzzle.

The full title of the painting *Caught in the Circle* is *The Last Stand* of *Three Troopers and a Scout Overtaken by a Band of Hostile Indians*. It was reproduced for the *Done in the Open* portfolio in 1903 and measures 12¼ inches by 19¾ inches with a fold, as a black and white "common man's" reproduction of the oil.

Thus we know there were inexpensive black and white versions of *Caught*. Can we find any inexpensive period (of the artist's lifetime) color prints as well?

*Caught in the Circle* was published again by Collier as a color halftone portfolio in 1908, entitled *Remington's Four Best Paintings*. And, voila: we have proved a student would have had the (inexpensive) material from which to try his hand at *Caught*.

If you think this is a unique occurrence for an appraiser, it is not. Many clients bring in all kinds of fake masterpieces. This "copy technique" is not far-fetched. Just go to www.reproduction-gallery .com which advertises that it will produce an oil copy of any painting, *any* size, for around $500. Art reproduction of originals is a shadowy business and, under U.S. law, often times illegal.

Yet I hammer home the point that work is sometimes reproduced *with* artists' signatures. Why should this hypothetical student not be prosecuted for signing Remington's name? Because some faked works do not intend to deceive; they are learning tools created by innocents in good faith while fraudulent works are meant to deceive.

What was my next step? To check with the National Cowboy and Western Heritage Museum, one of the best for Remington research.

It holds one of the few copies of Remington's *catalogue raisonné*, a tome most artists use to document their body of work and pinpoint the location, size, and medium of every painting in collections and to source the artist's own records. Not all artists were as aware of the market nor as organized as Remington was. In the end, the museum agreed that my client's painting was merely a good copy.

Now what if this client had seen the image for sale online, and then taken the chance that he was buying an original? Today, when so many pieces are available for purchase online and there's no chance for first-hand inspection, my advice is do not buy.

Wait until you can actually see it and smell it. Examine both best-case and worst-case scenarios. Drill down by adhering to my step-by-step formula to reason deductively before judging.

# A PATH INTO THE PAINTINGS OF

# PARIS

A FAVORITE OF MINE IS GRAND TOUR ART from young collectors: Parisian street paintings, collected in the late 19th and early 20th centuries by young, wealthy tourists. (Venetian street scenes were almost as popular.) A good example of high-end Parisian art is the street scenes of the glittering *City of Lights* painted by Edouard Cortès (1882–1969). In 2008, a lost Cortès painting of a Paris street scene was discovered among donated items at a Goodwill in Maryland. After an alert store manager noticed it as a signed original, the painting was subsequently auctioned for $40,600 at Sotheby's. Most street scenes are not as valuable, so when my client W.N. sent me a photo of two Paris street scenes, I yawned. But hang on! Some Parisian street scene paintings do indeed have value and this is a story of two such finds. This case study illustrates the

Paul Reynard *(David Heald)*. Inset: Poster, Paris Decorative Arts Show, 1924. In 1953 to 1955, Reynard designed the show.

*importance of researching a particular painting's genre.*

W.N.'s paintings were languishing on Etsy (www.etsy.com), a popular site for selling handmade goods. W.N. hoped to get $200 to $300 each, when a kind soul emailed that the price was too low. They had been painted by a certain Paul Reynard (aka "Renard") so W.N. pulled them and called me. Reynard was a French-born painter who had taught for 30 years at New York's School of Visual Arts, from 1981 to 2002. Reynard was also a glass artist, like his compatriot Marc Chagall, and created stained glass windows for notable French cathedrals. My favorite Chagall window is at the Art Institute of Chicago.

Reynard was also a muralist for some swanky addresses on Park Avenue and for Harvard. He had a most interesting relationship with Armenian mystic G.I. Gurdjieff, the creator of the School of the Fourth Way. Gurdjieff taught Four Ways for humans to stop "sleep walking" and raise consciousness. He maintained that the first Three Ways are the well-trodden monastic paths of yogis, monks, and fakirs. In other words, Gurdjieff taught the meditative life, the aesthetic life, and the simple life, as the Three Ways to clarity. But the Fourth Way was his own philosophical signature and diagram for living a conscious life. Gurdjieff's real masterwork was the discovery of "self-remembering": one must be mindful of both one's outside experiences and one's inner feelings and push away negativity.

Reynard was a staunch supporter of Gurdjieff and one can sense an element of mysticism in W.N.'s street scene painting.

This case study points out the *value of researching an artist's personal life* and I was able to pinpoint Reynard's great affection for the nostalgia of his Paris youth. These dreamy canvases found favor with his circle of philosophical admirers. These two canvases of W.N. are worth just under $2,000 each.

## AUSTRALIAN DREAM

# PAINTING

My CLIENT J.S. SENT ME TWO "DOTTED" paintings with what she described as illegible signatures. I asked her to bring one into my office because I couldn't identify the medium. Was it gouache? Gouache is a heavy, opaque watercolor paint made from natural umbers and ochers or metal compounds such as titanium, cobalt, and cadmium. When I saw this painting, there was evidence of traditionally-made gouache colors, with its predominance of pale yellow to dark reddish-brown ocher, which is derived from rock containing iron oxide. This case study emphasizes the *importance of researching a particular painting's style.*

The painting was a truly excellent example of Australian Aboriginal contemporary art. Although an ancient tradition, this technique was rediscovered by the art world in the early 1970s, and its rebirth occurred at a remote schoolhouse studio in the barren western desert of Australia. Dreaming Art, the cultural pride of Aboriginal communities, is perhaps the last great art movement of the 20th century, or so says my favorite art critic, Robert

Left: Mungo Man, New South Wales
(James Maurice Bowler)
Opposite: Grand Palais, Paris
(Vincent Desjardins)

*gwion-gwion* was painted in red on rock overhangs and in ancient caves. This bird is one of the originals of the blood-from-stone myth. The *gwion-gwion* pecks at these rocks looking for its insect meals so hard that it draws blood. I use the term "draws blood" in both meanings of the word "draw." Red ocher for these desert peoples symbolizes both the liquid blood of ancestors as well as the act of drawing.

Here's evidence of just how old the style is: it exists in archaeological sites at Lake Mungo in New South Wales, where blood-red pits hold red ocher-painted bones from the dead which have stained the ground pink. One of the most important historic finds is possibly the earliest human funerary site, from 40,000 to 55,000 years ago.

This is evidence of ancient artists' use of ocher mineral pigments and suggests that rock art was practiced from the beginning of Aboriginal civilization. The stenciled images of boomerangs, ancestor totems, and human hands are some of the oldest images in art history. Natural ocher pigments were used for burials, cave paintings, objects, and body art, and are still used today. So J.S., your $10 painting is worth $10,000 to $12,000.

Hughes. J.S.'s painting was found at a Catholic Charities Thrift Store in Santa Barbara—she bought it for $10! Many people cannot identify this distinctive style, let alone imagine its rarity (J.S. assumed it was a kid's piece). Today 5,000 to 7,000 Aboriginal people are known as studio artists working in the Dreaming style.

One reason I could not identify the paint medium by photo is because the traditional three- or four-colored ocher powders from the Dreaming land are mixed with real blood (human or kangaroo) and saliva. This intense blood red is hugely important in their works as well as in the funeral practices of the Aboriginal community. An example of such an ancient image is in West Kimberley. Thousands of years ago, the ancient totem of a bird-man called the

# BIG BUCKS

A CLIENT'S FATHER ASKED HER TO SEND
me a photo of a 20-by-24-inch oil on canvas. It's signed on the back by
Grigori Gluckmann (Grigori Efimovich Gluckmann, Russian, 1898-1973).
M.V. said the gallery label is dated 28-5-30, but Europeans transpose the
day and month so it's May 28, 1930. This is not just any gallery label: the
label reads Salon des Tuileries, 1930, and this oil-on-canvas bears the title
*Composition*. And the Salon des Tuileries is not just any gallery! This case
study instructs on *researching the time or era of the painting as well as the locale
or venue of an artist's showings.*

Gluckmann studied classical painting at the Moscow École des Beaux
Arts. He was caught up in the Russian Revolution and escaped to Germany,
but when Germany got too hot for a Jew, he left to study the Renaissance
masters in Italy. Landing in Paris in 1924, Gluckmann's work was picked
up by the famous Galerie Druet on the Rue Royale. His paintings are
well-composed and easily read, more realistic than expressionist, and usually

involve female nudes, female dancers, or musicians. The next year, in 1925, Gluckmann broke Paris wide open with his great work at the Big Three shows: the *Salon des Tuileries*, the *Salon d'Automne*, and *Salon National des Beaux Arts*. Thereafter he showed and sold in London and New York. Like many other artists trained in Moscow, Gluckmann developed a style that did not rely on a canvas. Canvas was hard to find in early 20th-century Russia, so he developed a technique of painting in layers on wood, which softens shapes and lines and lends itself perfectly to the female form.

A lot was going on in art when Gluckmann painted my client's oil. The most famous modern show was the *Société des Artistes Décorateurs* at Exposition 1930 in Paris's Grand Palais. Also in 1930 was the *Salon de l'École Française*, the *December Salon d'Automne*, and the *Salon Société des Artistes Indépendants*, as well as the *Congrès International d'Archéologie*, and the *Salon des Femmes Peintres et Sculpteurs*. 1930 was definitely a fertile year, as was 1934, when he had a solo Paris exhibition at Galerie Charpentier. That was when he befriended the renowned violinist Jascha Heifetz who introduced him to the world of the concert stage. The title of M.V.'s oil, *Composition*, refers to a group of dancers in a circular composition. This friendship was truly formative for Gluckmann and he much preferred the company of musicians and intellectuals to his fellow painters.

He continued the French tradition of painting the female form in Parisian nightlife but that came to an abrupt end during Germany's occupation of Paris. In 1941, he immigrated to New York and continued to show during the war.

Like so many Jewish European intellectuals of the mid-1940s, he ended up in Los Angeles, California. There he sold to celebrity clients of the Dalzell Hatfield Galleries in the swank Ambassador Hotel on Wilshire Boulevard. Later, in 1954, Gluckmann returned to paint Paris one more time and then showed at the Galerie Drouant-David. He then returned to Los Angeles and became an American citizen.

I found the sales figures for three other paintings by Gluckmann. In 2009, Sotheby's auctioned off *Before the Performance* (12 by 20 inches) for $35,000 and sold *Backstage* (35 by 27 inches) for $59,375. *Femme Nu* (13 by 16 inches), a full nude, sold more recently at Skinner's for $27,255. M.V. told her Dad the estimated value of his painting was between $25,000 and $35,000.

# ROMANTIC

A WOMAN SENT A PAINTING FROM HER
German grandmother that measured 26 by 20 inches. From the way the
light bounced off the painting, it was definitely an oil and the rough thread
patches below the oil appeared in the camera's flash. The canvas needed to be
re-stretched as the canvas tension was not uniform (not good for paint over
time). The owner said she couldn't see a signature. I'd asked that she remove
the frame and search for a signature because signatures can often determine
value. Nonetheless, I could deduce a few things about this piece without even
knowing the artist. This case study involves the *importance of familiarity with
the style of an era.*

First, the oil painting falls into that syrupy, late 19th-century romantic
period, which cherished depictions of aristocrats, the kings, and their courts.
The monarchy, as it was known for 1,000 years, was dying out. Dancing was
a common motif and painters' portrayals catered to the social tastes of the

as a throwback to an ancient past. This spirit of nostalgia and the glorified pomp-romp of formal settings seeped into art, with images of sweet, young, nubile maidens and soldier-suitors painted in candy-box colors. I'd bet the artist was a sentimental German, more so because the grandmother from whom my client inherited the painting was also German.

This overly-sweet style was still popular in Germany until WWI. So I deduced that the painting was probably done around 1890. At auction, this style and period of German art invariably lacks many bidders. But no doubt the style will grow in popularity.

During this era artists from all over Europe worked in a realistic style but with a hidden eroticism, a quality most desirable in select English painters. Consider the work of the pre-Raphaelites, whose paintings the common man can't touch today since their market value has skyrocketed. (Andrew Lloyd Webber collects them.)

For insurance purposes, I'd place the value of this work at $2,000 to $3,000. But if the owner sold today, she may actually only realize $300 to $400.

time. In this case, from the period of the Franco-Prussian War, when the Germans were flexing their muscle and attempting to take over parts of Europe which didn't belong to them, the French surely didn't approve.

All of Germany seemed to long for a monarch who reigned all-powerful. The German zeitgeist defiantly looked back to an era echoing classical history, which was even evident in their military uniforms. Pointed, short spikes rose from atop helmets

## ONE ARTIST'S MONEYMAKER:
# GICLÉE

I WAS SENT A FRAMED IMAGE OF A NATIVE
American mother and child (*Navajo Madonna*) signed DeGrazia. Yes, signed, and yes, it felt like a painted surface. But no, it was not a painting. It was a print that had been overlaid with texture. The signature was *in* the print covered by a glaze and hadn't been added later, so I knew this to be a copy of an original by Ettore "Ted" DeGrazia. This was a *giclée*, a French term meaning a photomechanical copy of an original work of art, executed in multiple (and sometimes unnumbered) editions (copies). A clue to DeGrazia's commercial success is that his Gallery in the Sun is listed on the National Register of Historic Places. This case study points out the *importance of determining if a work of art is commercially valuable rather than artistically valuable* (a work can fall into *both* categories).

So what made DeGrazia's work so popular and ubiquitous? DeGrazia was a natural marketer and networker back in the 1940s, and his good looks and confidence contributed to his success. He made the right connections in Scottsdale, Arizona, by befriending Alvin Lee "Buck" Saunders a civil engineer. Buck's artistically inclined wife, Leobarda, joined Saunders in opening the very first Scottsdale art gallery in March, 1949. It was simply called the Scottsdale Trading Post. This was far before Scottsdale became incorporated and far in advance of an average home price of $600,000.

If Scottsdale had been tonier in 1949, Buck and Leobarda probably wouldn't have named the first art gallery a simple trading post. But Leobarda stuck with the Trading Post, working there for 50 years until she died in 1999.

Buck Saunders was an avid fan of accessible art and a sentimentalist. He was fond of DeGrazia, also a romantic sentimentalist. Although he was of Italian descent, DeGrazia identified with the Arizona Native Americans of his time. He became fascinated with the Navajo tribe in 1930, painting Navajo waifs who herded sheep on their barren reservation. Conditions on the poor reservation during this period were dire and those children were likely starving. As for herding sheep and other animals, the Livestock Reduction Act of 1932 sanctioned the killing of 80% of the livestock

on the reservation of the Diné. The act considered the livestock mere family animals and unimportant. So bad was 1930 to 1940 for the Navajo Nation that it is now considered the Second Long Walk—the first being when they were paraded at gunpoint into New Mexico in 1864.

Any notion of innocent serenity was wholly a figment of his fertile imagination. Perhaps DeGrazia identified with the otherness of the Navajo people. He too had come from a small town and was an immigrant. He loved the Navajo child motif, and in the mountains outside of Tucson he built a studio and gallery modeled on the Mexican hacienda. He decorated it with romanticized images of Mexican and Indian children. The purity of their lives before the infiltration of white civilization fascinated him but he overlooked an important reality—that the white man had infiltrated long before.

Saunders gave DeGrazia his first one-man show at the Trading Post in 1951, and DeGrazia's autobiography calls it a smashing success. On the heels of this, he was then inspired to go to New York and pursue several other commercial avenues: textile design, decals, collector's

plates, needlepoint, key chains, greeting cards, children's books, prints, giclées, and serigraphs. This artist who celebrated purity then plunged head first into commercialism.

In the 1960s, UNICEF commissioned a Christmas card from him, which he called *Los Niños*: it was another depiction of Native American children and it sold five million boxes (a big deal at that time). His autobiography states he was unhappy being away from his beloved Indian subject matter. New York's pace caught up with him, and prompted his return to Arizona despite the huge success in New York.

Ted DeGrazia's *New York Times* obituary of September, 1982, states he made headlines in 1976 when he rode horseback with pack mules into the rugged Superstition Mountains of central Arizona to burn 100 paintings in protest of U.S. tax laws: "Mr. DeGrazia said he burned [his paintings] because the IRS, in comparing his work with [DeGrazia's] market value, made him 'A millionaire on paper...'." But DeGrazia was quoted as saying, "My heirs will have to pay . . . for which there is no money." And to make matters more interesting, the *Tucson Citizen* of January, 2011, stated that among the 10 horsemen who witnessed the DeGrazia painting bonfire of 1976, two of them (now in their dotage) claimed DeGrazia had entrusted them with secret knowledge of the burial site of 18 of the paintings. The two old gents claimed they're worth an aggregate of $18 million and that the paintings had been hermetically sealed and buried in the mountains.

The image belonging to my client is a print that's worth between $30 and $100, depending upon to whom she sells. I end with the *Tucson Citizen's* report on DeGrazia's next effort at making a low-budget Western film entitled *The End of the Rainbow*. It starred none other than DeGrazia himself, together with a posse as they locate treasure in the Superstition Mountains. That treasure is disclosed to be a hoard of DeGrazia's own paintings, which he slashes.

## REFLECTIONS & ILLUSIONS IN

# PORTRAITS

Let's switch our art historian hats to delve into the history of portraiture. This case study underlines the *importance of recognizing the genre or category of a work's subject matter*. Self-portraits were not even contemplated in Northern Europe until the 16th century. Artists themselves were not considered special: they were simple tradesmen, craftsmen and artisans, in the same class as masons and glaziers, and no one would have purchased an artist's self-portrait. However, many artists inserted their image into works and are quite recognizable. See Van Eyck's famous *Arnolfini Wedding Portrait:* the view in the mirror shows two figures just inside the door facing the couple. The second figure, in red, is presumably the artist, although unlike Velázquez in *Las Meninas*, he does not seem to be painting. The use of the mirror reflects the space and the portrait is unique as a record of a marriage contract in painting form.

The first self-portrait was by 13-year-old Albrecht Dürer in Nuremberg. Dürer was surely the greatest of Northern Renaissance artists and he continued to paint and produce woodcuts throughout his life.

In some portraits he appears Christ-like, and this was no accident. Dürer intended that we see him as the creator, just like the Creator, and these self-portraits seem to confirm the artist as a vessel for God's creativity.

At right is a painting on a wood panel painted early in 1500, just before his 29th birthday. It's the last of his three painted self-portraits and considered the most personal, iconic, and complex of his self-portraits.

Some portraits are valuable by virtue of the artist's skill and some by the sitter's celebrity (and sometimes both).

Above: Velázquez, *Las Meninas*
Below: Dürer, *Self-Portrait*

## FRAUDULENT PAINTINGS, PRINTS AND

# THEFT

A CLIENT WROTE THAT HER WORKPLACE, a residence for the elderly, was recently stripped of two Warhol screen prints. She wrote that there was no appraisal, and, until she and I had discussed value, there'd been no police report. The thieves had placed the works one at a time in a closet and waited until everyone became accustomed to the blank walls. Then they quietly made off with the Warhols.

This case study is a *warning regarding stolen, fake, and fraudulent art*. London's National Gallery mounted a show called *Close Examination: Fakes, Mistakes and Discoveries*. The National Gallery maintains a scientific department and is world famous in the study and techniques of Western European paintings. They displayed 40 paintings intended to deceive. Some were modified, some stolen and recovered, some wrongly attributed, and some executed by great, yet unknown, painters. These were not obscure painters: these were the National Gallery's Botticellis, Raphaels, Dürers, Gossaerts, Holbeins, and Rembrandts.

Portraits, in particular, are a huge playground for fraud. Years ago, the National Gallery had purchased what it thought was a 15th-century Renaissance portrait but recent analyses exposed a deception. The painter had used pigments which were unavailable prior to the 19th century and the paint was coated with resin to imitate age. One wonders just how many museum pieces are not as their label claims.

An interesting case study is that of a busty portrait entitled *Woman at a Window* (1510–1530) which was drastically over-painted in the 19th century to satisfy the Victorian era's modesty issues. Her cleavage was completely painted over, her blond hair changed to brown, her gown made modest, and her face enhanced to be more angelic and less beguiling. This is not uncommon. I own a 17th-century Italian landscape after Lorraine, with cows added to the foreground for display in the days of English country mansions, which always included a herd.

Over-painting is often a technique intended to deceive. The National Gallery bought what it thought was an actual Holbein in 1990, but when viewed under a microscope, the over-painting revealed it was not a Holbein.

The painting was from the 15th century (the right period for a Holbein) but the distinctive cap had been over-painted to copy a Holbein-style headdress. Often the canvas or wood panel upon which a painting sits can be too early or too late to have been used by the painter as attributed.

Clients occasionally ask why two figures in an early painting appear as if painted by different hands. The answer is simple: they were. It is quite impossible to recreate the workings of an Old Master's studio because the Master may have painted the focal image of a piece, while his assistants may have painted in backgrounds and other figures.

Sometimes the Master left the most important element in a painting to his assistant, just to see if he could carry it off. Other times, the assistant himself started as a lowly background painter and then surpassed his Master—as did Botticelli and Leonardo da Vinci, both of whom Andrea del Verrocchio tutored in the 15th century.

A particularly tricky strategy is for a great forger to paint what would naturally be seen as a mate to an existing Master's piece. For example, take the clever forger who studied Botticelli's *Venus* and knocked off a *Mars*, claiming that it was Venus's

companion. The National Gallery has both, hanging side by side.

But we have good news. Some beautiful works by authenticated painters have been discovered: Raphael's *Madonna of the Pinks*, for example. Raphael didn't like his work and painted over it, making it what is deemed today as inferior.

Caravaggio's gigantic painting the *Kiss of Judas* (1603) was luckily recovered on a street in Berlin. Four Ukrainians had stolen the $100 million work in July of 2008 by cutting a window in the poorly-secured Odessa Museum of Western and Eastern Art. They then cut the Caravaggio out of its frame and, as they left, scattered boxes of nails on the exit road to flatten police tires.

Believe it or not, the men had a potential buyer at $100 million, who was also arrested. After spending $100 million, how could someone hope to display the stolen art? In 2005, five years after the 1630 Rembrandt *Self-Portrait* was stolen from Sweden's National Museum in Stockholm, the Danish police recovered it. Eight men had found a buyer who was about to pay millions for the iconic piece.

*A particularly tricky stategy is for a great forger to paint what would be seen as a mate to an existing Master's piece... take the clever forger who studied Botticelli's Venus and knocked off a Mars...*

They were all arrested in 2005 in a Copenhagen hotel room while still haggling. Again, where can one display a stolen Rembrandt? If you plan to buy a painting, research its provenance, its ownership history. More about how to research provenance is in the chapter "Looting of Antiquities Today."

## A TALE OF

# FORGERY

$T$HE CLIENT CAME INTO THE OFFICE WITH a lovely oil painting signed A.G. Deacon. This case study focuses on the *purchase of frauds and the distinction between fraud and forgery.* This oil-on-canvas landscape depicted a scenic French vineyard and came with a font of memories, as do many works. When T.T. was 22 back in 1976, he roamed Britain on a shoestring and finally found cheap quarters near Hyde Park where he signed up a roommate to save money. This roommate, A.G., was a middle-aged British painter who sold at a market stall in Hyde Park and bragged that he could forge anyone's brushstrokes. T.T. cautioned A.G. that forging paintings is risky business. A.G. had quite a nice canvas hanging in their shared room, and T.T. liked it so well that he bought it for $350. And that's the painting T.T. brought in for me.

T.T. received letters from A.G. for years after, and A.G.'s signatures often sported different names and different spellings. Unsurprisingly, A.G.

was eventually found out as an artist's fraudster and sent to jail. This explains why I couldn't find any sales records for paintings by an A.G. Deacon. T.T.'s painting reminds me of a Rudyard Kipling poem "The Conundrum of the Workshops," in which the Devil asks the artist, "You did it, but was it art?"

The story of forged art is never more interesting than these two famous British cases: the first one involves a mid-19th-century cult known as the Transformationalists.

This community was simply hellbent on transforming the world through all the arts. They believed that the arts have no authorship since everyone is an artist. Not surprisingly, a great forger emerged from this circle, a Malcolm Bingham, who was later shot by an unhappy art collector in 1904. That violent act perhaps reveals more beyond his devious talent: he was ruining the market!

The second case is more recent but equally strange; this one revolves around a 20th-century ingenious (and damaging) art scammer. Genius forger John Myatt was sentenced to prison in England in the mid-1990s for forging a slew of works, including Marc Chagall, Georges Braque, Dubuffet, Henri Matisse,

Giacometti, Ben Nicholson, and Le Corbusier, all from his pretty cottage outside of London. Myatt had painted 200 forgeries in the styles of nine modern masters while delivering a painting every six weeks to a John Drewe, his accomplice and marketer. Drewe consigned these 200 works to Christie's, Sotheby's, and Phillips, as well as very reputable dealers throughout London, Paris, and New York. Myatt earned over $165,000 during that time, all stashed in a Swiss bank account.

Drewe had "authenticated" these works via bogus provenances he'd created and he attained access to the tightest security art archives in the world while establishing a chain of ownership and a history of the works (along with stolen "official" authenticating seals). Of the 200 "masterworks" by Myatt which Drewe sold in the market, only 73 of them have actually been recovered or located. The rest are still out there — 127 fakes! Drewe surely capitalized on the art world's reliance on provenance and methods of validation. Myatt knew how to paint. Drewe knew how to manipulate the system: it was a nearly perfect scam.

Forgers like Deacon, Drewe, and Myatt create a fiction and adopt many personas and professions. John

Drewe, for example, was born John Cockett.

At any given point, he was a Ph.D. professor of physics, a descendant of the Earl of York, a functionary in the Ministry of Defence, and even associated with the MI6, British Intelligence. In real life, Myatt was a recently divorced art teacher who was in desperate need. The writer Peter Landesman, who covers forgeries in the art world, wrote that "perhaps no better forger of his or any other time has worked so prodigiously and in so many styles."

One wonders how many of our museums' collections are genuine. Thomas Hoving, former director of New York's Metropolitan Museum of Art, said during his tenure a full 40% of the works considered for purchase by the Met were phony or over-restored. Artists are not

blameless: Salvador Dalí on his deathbed signed thousands of sheets of blank paper for future fake etchings and lithographs.

As long as the market pays big bucks, people will commit fraud. When I applied for graduate student research at the Victoria and Albert National Art Library, I was required to provide a scholarly reference letter. John Drewe had also researched there, and when he applied, stated his occupation as physics professor. He concocted a new persona to be a reference, a Dr. John Cockett (one of many aliases), and used his actual address. When the Library wrote to the address, Drewe wrote back "John Drewe is a man of integrity," and signed it "Dr. John Cockett."

What cheek! So, T.T.'s painting is worth a great story but, alas, not a great deal of money.

## WHEN A FAKE ISN'T
# FRAUD

WHEN IS A FAKE NOT REALLY A FORGERY?
This case study draws the vital *distinction between paintings intended to defraud and paintings (as in the previous Remington case study) created as fakes or reproductions, and how to research fraud.* The art world's definition of a fake is that a forgery can be a fake, but if the artist has no intention of causing financial harm, a fake can serve other purposes. It can be a learning tool, a gift for someone who can't afford the original, or a student's re-creation in imitation of another artist's style. A forgery is a fraud when it's intended to defraud, either by co-opting an idea or by charging money with a false claim of authorship. If a fake, the artist admits to copying but never copies for profit. If a fraud, an artist hopes no one will realize the representation isn't by the claimed artist, and so intent and motive to produce a copy are quite different.

A.N.'s lithograph, which she had owned for 30-odd years, is in the

Left: Victoria and Albert National Art Library *(Wuselig)*
Above: Dufy, *Le Cavalier arabe*, 1901

style of Raoul Dufy (1877–1953), a renowned Fauvist (colorist) post-impressionist painter. Dufy loved to paint water of all kinds, from seaports to bathwater. He also loved to paint bathing nudes for which, like all great sensuous activities, the French have a word: *baigneuses* ("nude bathers"). A.N.'s lithograph by Montfort has happy, bare French bathers, a lot like Dufy's. The very loose, sketchy style and palette are very similar to Dufy's, yet the work is signed Montfort. Therefore, we have an interesting degree of fakery. The work is signed by one artist but it's almost a dead ringer for the style, palette, and themes of a much better-known artist. Montfort wised up, but not completely. Jean-Jacques Montfort eventually just parodied art, but in 1960 he was sent to France's Fresnes Prison for forging a painting in the style of Maurice de Vlaminck (French, 1876–1958). He had "unintentionally" sold it at auction in 1960 for $40,000.

When A.N. bought her lithograph in 1978, Montfort was just out of jail and had decided to move to Beverly Hills and paint again. He did admit (perhaps merely for publicity's sake) that he was a "master parodist," meaning a fraud turned innocent faker. Montfort said he created *faux-faux*—"fake-fakes."

His work was sold out of the Phyllis Morris Design Studio in Beverly Hills. By this time, those in the art market knew if they bought a Montfort they were buying a legitimate fake. It's not illegal to paint in someone else's style if you sign your own name. When asked why he wanted to paint in the style of the likes of Picasso, Dufy, Braque, and Chagall for eventual sale, Montfort reported to *People Magazine* in December, 1978, that he "wanted [his] old friends to meet together at the stump of [his] brushes, to walk together and know each other." Nice.

In 1978, he sold works like A.N.'s for between $15 and $25. He's not the only forger to turn legit. A capitalist to the bone, Jean-Jacques Montfort was bold enough to title his autobiography *Emballez c'est signe: les tribulations d'un faussaire*, which translates as *The Tribulations of a Faker*. It was published in 2003 (French edition only) by Fayard and is a long 300 pages. A friend has kindly translated Montfort's defense as: "I am a faker of art, something one doesn't find in professional registers. It's true that we are not many [in] modern art. The orientation [faker] is too marginal, [and] sounds a lot like a swindler's work, when it doesn't fall into outright fraud. So, now that my book is finished and I

*I am a faker of art... now that my book is finished... I feel a little loony, almost senile, for agreeing to bare my revelations, embarking you on the road that took me from the Latin Quarter (Paris) to Beverly Hills, without forgetting the stop in Fresnes [jail]... So, lifting the veil from the mirror that swings from real to fake, one discovers the art market for what it is: a great Punch-and-Judy show.*

—Jean-Jacques Montfort

the ex-wife of another great French forger known as David Stein, who entitled her book *Three Picassos Before Breakfast: Memoirs of an Art Forger's Wife,* which is a compilation of their shared history published in 1973.

Mr. Stein did a long stretch in France's Fresnes prison as well, and was released from prison only to sell fakes which, like Mr. Montfort, he signed with his own name. The value of A.N.'s lithograph? Here's the vengeance of the art market: sales of Montfort's works were not recorded for public record like other well-known original works, so A.N.'s lithograph just adds up to a juicy story in the history of art. And, unfortunately, it's only worth the paper it's faked on.

can look at its pages, I feel a little loony, almost senile, for agreeing to bare my revelations, embarking you on the road that took me from the Latin Quarter (Paris) to Beverly Hills, without forgetting the stop in Fresnes [jail]. It may give the impression of not wanting to budge from similar activities.

"Anyway, I feel a little like Arsène Lupin (the French detective, à la Sherlock Holmes) in this dirty affair. So, lifting the veil from the mirror that swings from real to fake, one discovers the art market for what it is: a great Punch-and-Judy show."

Along similar lines, there's also a book written by Anne-Marie Stein,

## FAKE PRINTS: DON'T GET

# SWINDLED

I WAS SO IMPRESSED TO SEE REPORTED IN the *Financial Times* a story about my special world, the authentication of fine art prints. You would be stunned at the number of fake Salvador Dalí prints I've come across—and I have the sorely disappointed clients to prove it. Dalí holds the unenviable position of being one of the most faked artists of all time. I'll give you a big hint about how to spot a reproduced print: it's all about the dots! This case study serves as an *excellent guide for buying and evaluating works of art on paper.*

The situation has gotten out of hand, so much so that that new laws have been enacted in an attempt to protect art collectors. It used to be "buyer beware" but then, in a total reversal it's become "seller beware." Still, one must be on guard when buying prints. I especially caution clients not to buy them on cruise ships, as cruise ship companies are often in cahoots with large commercial art dealers. Since passengers are a captive audience, dealers may hold an art auction on the ship and the art will have a seal of authentication from this dealer. Almost all cruise ships which sell art this way are selling mere reproductions of original prints. It's difficult to tell if a print is reproduced (especially when one is rolling on the high seas), but here are some hints:

- If an artist is dead, famous, and modern, take it to an expert before purchasing it.
- Bring a small magnifying glass with you and if you see dots under magnification it's probably a fake. Original etchings, engravings, and lithographs will never exhibit a dot-matrix pattern.
- Beware of prints by Salvador Dalí for two reasons. His is the art most faked and before he died, as a prank (he was a trickster), he signed thousands of blank sheets before they were printed. Not to mention that his signature is quite easily forged.
- Beware of prints marked in the margins with "EP" or "AP." This notation connotes that the prints are from the first strikes by the artist, before the run of an edition. They were done *before* the series was numbered. "Numbering" is a small fraction usually written in pencil to indicate the number of the print in the print run. Thus, if the artist has decided to print 100 images and you're looking at the 35th strike, your print will bear the fraction 35/100. The prints most often faked or forged will be signed "EP" (Exhibition Proofs) or "AP" (Artist's Proofs) because there's no way to know if that print was in the artist's chosen edition number. Practiced fakers don't falsify fractions because an artist's catalogue raisonné will state which print is in which collection.

- Beware of unsigned prints or prints signed *in the plate or in the stone*. An original print will be signed (usually in pencil) in the margins. Prints which are signed in the plate are signatures that are directly on the actual image. That means the artist had signed the print as part of the lithographic or engraving process. So if a faker has the artist's original engraving plate or lithographic stone, this is an easy restrike. I've even seen fake prints signed in the margins with reproduction signatures. You'll see that dot-matrix pattern again unless the forger was bold enough to write in the artist's signature.

- Beware of estate-signed prints, meaning that once an artist has died, the heirs sign the artist's name for the estate. These are not worth nearly as much as those the artist oversaw when alive.

- Beware of prints claiming to be "genuine limited editions." I've

Above: Display at Salon du Livre Ancien et de L'estampe, 2013, Grand Palais, Paris
*(Lionel Allorge)*

seen many "certificates of authenticity" with this common phrase. If a print is a genuine limited edition, there's no need to say it. A genuine limited edition print means the master etching, engraving, or lithograph stone is defaced after the print run is complete, to ensure no further copies will ever be made.

- Beware of prints that have a printer's business name in the margins or on the back. These are usually tops of calendars, cutouts, or mail-order da Vincis. A common printing house for reproduction prints is Collier's.

- Beware of prints, especially the Japanese woodcuts, which are cut right up to the image. Without a margin surrounding the image, one can't be certain it's an original.

Finally, there are millions of cheap prints to be found from the turn of the 19th century to 1940 due to the great popularity of art reproduction photography and the reproduction of masterworks by earlier artists. The American middle class loved to decorate parlors with these and they're difficult to identify because they look as old as the originals.

Remember to always check for the dot-matrix pattern here. I'm constantly amazed by TV shows such as *Pickers* and *Storage Wars* wherein someone finds a treasure worth $20,000. Also, a good print will almost always be printed on heavy, good quality stock.

The real odds of your print making a headline like "$5 Yard Sale Find Is Worth Five Million" is akin to winning the lottery: 14 million to one. But winning occasionally happens and the print market is boiling hot again so don't give up the hunt. There's still plenty of gold in them thar hills!

# VALUE

CLIENTS OFTEN ASK HOW TO CARE FOR
art and antiques and my advice is: don't mess with furniture or art. It's true
that a refinished 18th-century furniture piece will be devalued if the old finish
is removed but, strangely, the same advice may not hold for more common
late 19th-century pieces. Usually a damaged work of art or furniture will
not be worth as much as a perfect example unless it's so rare it retains its
value, which is usually a function of great age or provenance. This case study
imparts an *understanding of value with respect to condition, rarity, and the "story"*
*of an object, known as provenance.*

Several years ago, actor Dennis Hopper encountered quite a surprise. His
estate sold a Warhol screen print of Mao Tse-tung estimated at $20,000 to
$30,000. Amazingly, the piece jumped and sold for $302,500 at a Christie's
auction in January 2011. Why the incredible leap in price? Apparently, Mr.
Hopper came home late one night and believed his screen print of Mao

Tse-tung looked especially frightening: he grabbed his nearby pistol and shot two bullets into Mao's face. Andy Warhol was amused by this story and signed the holes, one called the "Warning Shot," and the other "Bullet Hole." In this case, the damage did not devalue the print; it only increased it.

Theft, of course, is another way to decrease value, though some famous art thefts have increased the notoriety of a recovered piece. A favorite story regards the *Mona Lisa* by da Vinci. It was stolen in August 1911 from the *Louvre* by employee Vincenzo Peruggia, who allegedly had the original masterpiece copied four times before it was finally found two years later. Art experts have never found the copies, leading some to speculate as to whether the lady at the *Louvre* is the original.

In 1934, two of the 12 panels of the glorious *Ghent Altarpiece* by the Van Eyck brothers were stolen by thief Arsène Goedertier. Although Goedertier had sent ransom letters, he died without any dough and the panels have never been found.

One of my appraiser colleagues in New York was an expert at a trial centering on the theft of a beautiful 16th-century German *Evangelistarum*, once the prize of the 19th-century Abbey of Quedlinburg. This is a Latin book on the Evangelists and the cover of the illuminated manuscript was decorated with gold, silver, and jewels. In 1945, during World War II, an American soldier, a Mr. Joe Meador, stole this irreplaceable volume. Then, while still in Europe, Joe simply mailed the treasure to his hometown of Whitewright, Texas, through the army post office. Few would've known about the theft: Joe had swiped the manuscript from a mineshaft cave used to hide looted Nazi spoils of war. Who would keep track of all the stolen goods? After returning from war, Joe kept it quietly on the bookshelf at his farm in Texas until he died in 1980.

A neighbor of Joe's, Frank Wornher, had rented a home from Joe, and found some cowboy boot boxes with Joe's letters describing the theft. After Joe's death, his relatives inherited the treasure and put it up for sale, whereupon the German government paid them over $2.75 million. But before turning it over to the German authorities, the same heirs sold part of the manuscript to another entity, even though they'd already accepted millions from the German government! A massive court battle ensued, the end result being that the statute

Above: Van Eyck (circa 1390-1441), *Ghent Altarpiece*

of limitations had expired, so theft charges were eventually dismissed. Ever vigilant, the trusty IRS got the husband and wife for capital gains, big time—$50 million! And the manuscript, which had been sold by Joe's brother, ended up purchased by an anonymous donor who then returned the priceless *Evangelistarum* to Germany.

The most valuable painting ever stolen was Vermeer's *The Concert*

from the Isabella Stewart Gardner Museum, Boston, in March, 1990. That day, thieves took 13 pieces of art, collectively worth $300 million. Not even one has ever been recovered and a reward still remains at five million dollars for information (be on the lookout). Missing pieces include a Vermeer, two Rembrandt oils, a Rembrandt self-portrait etching, a Manet, and five Degas paintings.

One of the saddest thefts involves

a Stéphane Breitwieser, a young man who traveled Europe in 2001 and stole 238 works of art from various museums. His reason? To build his and his mother's private collection back home. He only came clean in 2005 and was sentenced to 26 months in prison. Unfortunately, some of the works were never recovered because Breitwieser's mother, Mireille Stengel, chopped up 60 of the paintings in an effort to remove evidence. These included masterpieces: Brueghel, Watteau, Boucher, and de Lyon.

The most outlandish theft involved the huge 2005 heist of a two-ton bronze sculpture *Reclining Figure* (1969–1970) by Henry Moore from the Henry Moore Foundation's sculpture park in England. Thieves with a crane lifted the figure (just over three-and-a-half meters long, two meters high, and two meters wide) onto the back of a Mercedes trailer-truck. More amazing is that no one noticed it being hoisted. This irreplaceable behemoth has amazingly never been recovered. How do you hide a two-ton sculpture? Sadly, the Moore sculpture may already have been reduced to scrap.

If art theft still intrigues you, do look into these books: Robert K. Wittman's *Priceless: How I Went Undercover to Rescue the World's Stolen Treasures*, Ken Follett's novel *The Modigliani Scandal*, Miles Harvey's *The Island of Lost Maps: A True Story of Cartographic Crime*, Darian Leader's *Stealing the Mona Lisa: What Art Stops Us from Seeing*, Konstantin Akinsha's *Beautiful Loot: The Soviet Plunder of Europe's Art Treasures*, Robert Noah's novel *The Man Who Stole the Mona Lisa*, Anne-Marie Stein's *Three Picassos Before Breakfast: Memoirs of an Art Forger's Wife*, and William H. Honan's *Treasure Hunt: A New York Times Reporter Tracks the Quedlinburg Hoard*. I've chuckled over all these, and found that fact is indeed stranger than fiction.

## THE TEN MOST INSANE ART

# LOSSES

I N THE U.S. WE CAN ENJOY 8,000 MUSEUMS
holding our treasures in trust. The *International Council of Museums Directory* lists over 55,000 museums in 202 countries. That's a lot of safeguarding against human interference, natural disasters, war, theft, ignorance, and other varieties of destruction. Sadly, some works of art haven't been so lucky. The ones I describe are world famous but have been damaged due to carelessness, insanity, negligence, or anger. Rembrandt, da Vinci, Michelangelo, Picasso, Velázquez, and more have rolled in their graves as their masterpieces were attacked. This case study underlines the *necessity of documentation: keep notes and photographic records on valuable objects.*

Some historic cases of art loss are included here:

• Marcel Duchamp's urinal titled *Fountain* was tossed in the trash by its photographer, the famous Alfred Stieglitz.

- Rembrandt's *The Night Watch* (1642) a monumental 12 feet by 14 feet, has been furiously attacked three times at the Rijksmuseum. In 1911, an unemployed cook slashed it with his knife. In 1975, a schoolteacher slashed it repeatedly before guards hauled him back to the mental hospital, where he then committed suicide. In 1990, a man sprayed it with acid, perhaps because the subject is Rembrandt-era police!

- Rembrandt continues to get a lot of heat. His *Danaë* features a voluptuous nude in bed beckoning to Zeus. In 1985, at the Hermitage Museum in Leningrad, a deranged man stabbed the nude's crotch repeatedly and then, if that wasn't enough, doused the large 8-by-10-foot painting with acid. Full restoration took the Russians 12 years.

- It's not just men who attack nude females. In 1914, at the height of the suffragette movement in London, the female head of the British Union of Fascists warned The National Gallery that she was going to mount an attack on Velázquez's *Rokeby Venus* (1647). In spite of being warned, the Gallery didn't challenge her as she marched in and slashed the nude's back seven times. She was finally apprehended, resulting in just six months in the slammer.

- In 1987, a Briton angered by politics used a sawed-off shotgun to shoot at da Vinci's charcoal drawing *Virgin and Child with St. Anne and St. John the Baptist* (1499). The gun ripped a six-inch hole into it and restorers have never found all the pieces.

- The astounding *Roman Portland Vase* (30–20 BC) is almost 12 inches tall and the most famous and earliest blown cameo glass in history. It was found in 16th-century Rome and remained intact for almost 2,000 years until 1845 when a drunk heaved a neighboring sculpture on his back and hurled it atop the vase, smashing both artifacts. It's been restored four times since.

- The day I saw *The Little Mermaid* in Copenhagen was just after Christmas and bitterly cold, yet the four-foot bronze was still being admired by other fools. She's so famous and so small and accessible that she's been covered innumerable times with paint (name your color). She's been beheaded twice, each time necessitating a new head (thieves kept the old ones). Both arms have been sawed off and stolen and, in a political move, she was blasted off her rock with dynamite.

- One of the most memorable attacks was on Michelangelo's *Pietà* in 1498, when a man lunged at it with a hammer screaming "I am Jesus Christ!" This would-be Messiah did significant damage. Avaricious onlookers, meanwhile, immediately threw themselves to the floor, collecting shattered bits of marble for souvenirs. The Virgin Mary's nose was never recovered.
- How's this for museum fatigue? At New York's Metropolitan Museum of Art, a woman fainted onto Picasso's *The Actor* (1904), tearing into it in 2010. The cost of her fainting spell—a mere $130 million.
- Steve Wynn, the famous Las Vegas developer, loves to buy art and owns priceless paintings. Just as he was closing the deal on Picasso's *Le Rêve* (1932) for $139 million, he accidentally hit the painting and poked a hole in it with his elbow. The sale was off and Wynn coughed up $90,000 for its restoration.

In spite of these calamities, art is tenacious and we protect it as a symbol of its irreplaceable value. Finally, the relationship of stolen works to value may be summed up like this: if it's not there, it has no value. At the base of insuring your treasures is that *you* must prove ownership by documenting your objects. Shoot both *still photos* and *videos*, and include where your treasures are located (and even those who live among them). Then store these images outside of the house in an office or a safe-deposit box. This is very important, whether an object is stolen or your house burns down, because an insurance company wants proof of ownership beyond a receipt.

Finally, if a work of art is stolen, post an image of it on the Art Loss Register (www.artloss.com). That worthy organization is connected to Interpol, and it is also available to appraisers and museum curators. So one may get a stolen object returned in one piece (and without bullet holes).

NOSTALGIA

# GAMES

$M$Y FAMILY TOOK TERRIBLE VACATIONS.
For example, my father, Frank, and my mother, Elly, drove us in our mammoth, avocado-green station wagon all the way from our Illinois farm town to one of the most horrid places on the planet: the Lake of the Ozarks in Missouri. Every single summer they did this to us! It's the worst place because the lake was created by a major government-ordered flood in the 1920s. No matter how hot it was, we weren't allowed to swim because we'd probably get sucked under by an old, bottomed-out washing machine or impaled by a sharp, rusted farm implement. Plus, there were legions of leeches and snakes living in that lake. So the only things we could do during those summers were to sweat and play board games. This case study focuses on the *nostalgic value in the Collectibles marketplace.*

Now those 1980s board games are certainly making a cult collectible comeback. Go search under your beds for "Elizabeth's Worst 1980s Games," chosen for their value and rarity. We live in an age when we have 23 gaming systems on practically every TV, not to mention computer games played by one billion players worldwide. There's something so serene and innocent about the early gaming monstrosities, some of which had electronics (though primitive), as well as stiff mechanical tools, and three-dimensional structures.

From the least obnoxious game to the most, I begin with Number Nine, Operation, which has been in production since 1965. This game was my sadistic younger brother's favorite vacation game. I always hated the way the tweezers scraped the poor guy's metallic cut-out body (one's children may still be subjected to this perversity, as the game is still produced). Not only could you poke your sister's eye out with those tweezers (Paul tried), but if you couldn't remove the patient's appendix, the game bleated the most nail-grating alert when you ruptured his insides. If vintage, this game is worth $50.

At Number Eight is the vintage game Fireball Island. This rates because of its short production run. Its plastic god could kill you with fireballs and it also included great playing cards to help find the hidden diamond. My brother Paul poked holes in all the raised-mountain topography (and cheap plastic can splinter). It is now a real treasure so a 1986 game in good condition is worth $200 because most of them were destroyed by younger brothers.

I rate Connect Four as Number Seven. This game actually reflects the halcyon days of the 1980s when young people played this somewhat sophisticated version of tic-tac-toe. One lined up either red or black pieces in a tic-tac-toe line on a two-sided plastic rack. The best part (for the time) was a highly-engineered switch which flipped the rack over onto your opponent, acting as an automatic default. Then one re-racked and restarted. Today it's worth $45.

Paul was always a nerd and is currently a mechanical/electrical engineer (surprise!), so he loved choice Number Six, Electronic Battleship. The center of the game looked like a Houston Command control panel and was actually a rudimentary computer. Here's a true cultural masterpiece complete with beginning LEDs, whining explosive blasts, and very loud, scraping noises. Paul never actually played the game; he just ran the computer until one day he took it apart to see how it worked. This is why I no longer have it. If I did, I'd be $130 richer.

Number Five is Mouse Trap—one step up from playing gin rummy with our beloved skinny, nearly-blind Aunt Kathleen at the Lake of the Ozarks. The game was perfect for long afternoons by the stinky algae-choked lake. So much so that I forgot about the awful creepy rats invading our rustic motel. There were so many plastic parts needed to build that mouse trap on a pole (someone's baby always ate a few of those) that eventually we couldn't play. Today a nice one is worth $50.

My littlest brother, David, just loved Hungry Hungry Hippos and it's my Number Four. David didn't move the hippos on their sticks: he kicked at each of the obscenely-colored hippos with his shoe until out popped those little pink balls. Hungry Hungry Hippos in good shape is worth $75.

Paul loved to rattle the dice in the dome of my Number Three, Trouble. But he played the odds, not the game. Remember how one could hammer the bubble to make the dice annoyingly pop around? The bubble was called a Pop-O-Matic and one could easily embed a sharp piece of plastic into one's palm. Trouble sells for $50.

Aunt Kathleen and Uncle Gene and several of my cousins loved to gamble. And they always drove all the way from St. Ann, Missouri, to Lake of the Ozarks to suffer a summer vacation with our family. Inevitably, they brought along my Number Two, the hated game of Trivial Pursuit—a personal nightmare. My cousin Cecilia was a beautiful redhead, a chubby and bespectacled brainiac, who tossed her flaming mane every time she was correct. Which meant flying hair throughout the game. I hated trivia and once even tried burning the cards.

Finally, my title for The Very Worst Game of the 1980s goes to Wheel of Fortune with its million little plastic windows and stupid double wheel. Not even my mother, a crack bridge player, could figure out how to play this game. We only knew it was extremely fragile so we constantly tried to protect it from my little brother. If you recall, this plastic board game had slotted sections, as tall as buildings, which more often than not snapped off.

What fascinates me is not that the games are worth so much now but that nostalgia is what sharply drives up value in the Collectibles marketplace. And they've all been recreated in online versions—as if once weren't enough!

# SPACE AGE

Everything CREATED BY MAN HAS BEEN
new at one time, as these two items I describe will confirm. This case study
focuses on *collectibles which only yesterday were considered junk, as well as how to
predict future trends*. The first one resembles an outer space alien but is actually what we watched in 1955, if we had the money. It's the Philco Predicta
TV with an outlandish swiveling 15-inch screen attached to its base. The
dial has 13 numbers for channels (very wistful and hopeful in 1955 when at
most we had three). It also sports a push button on/off switch and three side
dials: controls for color, contrast, and snow. Compare this to today's TVs with
thousands of channels and buttons (often on three separate remotes) and
you get an idea of how much more the 1955 Philco Predicta TV evokes the
nostalgia for simpler times.

Our current TVs don't have vacuum tubes, but a Los Angeles client collected them. A confirmed bachelor, he made bank by selling these rarities to those with old TVs. Some paid hundreds for a rare vacuum tube since many collectors wanted to get those old cabinet radios and TVs in working order again.

This client found old vacuum tubes behind toolboxes in garages and would often discover one in a defunct radio and purchase the entire radio. He'd visit any garage sale that smelled of a deceased engineer's estate. Unfortunately, this Philco Predicta TV doesn't have a working vacuum tube so it's entirely inoperable, decreasing its value from $600 to $400. No tubee, no workee.

While we're on the subject of old vacuum tubes, let me explain why a first iteration of any new idea in material culture is valuable. As an example, let's start with the computer, which began with vacuum tubes. Back in 1943 during World War II, J. Presper Eckert and John Mauchly created the brain of the world's first computer, called the ENIAC (Electronic Numerical Integrator and Computer). When a part of this ENIAC, a decade ring counter, was offered at auction, it was the only component of the ENIAC known to be in private hands. The ring counter has a black steel chassis

with 27 of 28 vacuum tubes, 10 indicator light apertures, two male plugs on the exterior, and one outlet inside. Plus there are wires, busses, and connections. Yes, you guessed right: one vacuum tube is missing, and therefore it's inoperable.

The ENIAC was sold in Boston by Skinner's in 2000 at a one-day specialist auction of science and technology lots. (Included was a similar Philco Predicta.) Now here's the kicker: the ENIAC sold for almost $80,000, more than six times what the auction house estimated (see ENIAC in "Investments: the Best and Worst").

An interesting market phenomenon may occur when an object's class or category first becomes collectible, as with such "antique" computers today. When an object sells for six times what an auction house estimates, people will come forward to claim a piece of the "antique" electronics pie.

Other prototype computers are out there for the finding. Although scholarship on an early "first" computer names the inventors as Drs. John Maunchly and J. Presper Eckert, other scholars point to a parallel team of inventors at Iowa State University. Drs. Clifford Berry and John Vincent Atanasoff were also credited with work on the early frontiers of binary memory. Dr. Berry, according to the book *Atanasoff: Forgotten Father of the Computer*, had thought of the idea for binary memory when he was a 21-year-old doctoral candidate. Atanasoff and Berry's computer was named the ABC but there was an issue with its patent. Sadly, Dr. Berry took his life in 1963 in a New York hotel room, but not before he made a little vacuum tube monaural phonograph player for his great niece (a client of mine and owner of valuable early technological documents). Which brings us to a new collectible category: obsolete machines that are now rare and desirable. Some vintage record players (aka "phonographs" for those my age) are actually worth something. For example, I owned one of those little pink, plastic record players we dragged to slumber parties in Deerfield, Illinois. The turntable was in the "suitcase" along with a speaker and electric cord, and it weighed a ton. Compare that to the iPod! But then the bigger and chunkier the record player or boom box, the cooler you were. An art deco aluminum case with front speaker grill may bring as much as $2,500. A few years ago, one was featured in the Brooklyn Museum show *The Machine Age*, exhibited as sculpture!

The collectible market is seeing a strong interest in vinyl records, along with LP album covers, 45 covers, and paper sleeves. Some of the values for sleeves will make you wish you had saved yours. One collector emailed me that he had a sleeve without the record of Bruce Springsteen's *Blinded by the Light* from 1973 (Columbia 45805). The owner asked me if he should toss it since he'd lost the record (don't throw those paper sleeves away). Sure, it's only for a 45 record, but at auction it could bring $500 if it's the Boss's rarest sleeve. The collecting of old vinyl is truly a sleuther's field as there's so much vinyl at garage sales.

Which vinyl records are money-makers? A collector has a 78 recording from 1924 by Ma Rainey performing "Lost Wandering Blues" (Paramount 12098). The record is barely playable but because it's Ma Rainey's first record after signing her recording contract, it's worth $200. Look for the rare ones, for instance, *Mean When I'm Mad* (don't you love that title?) by Eddie Cochran, 1957 (Liberty 55070). It's worth $600.

Here is an illustration about vinyl rarity. Both Elvis's and the Beatles' recordings are hardly considered rare. But the records that jump-started their careers are. I have a sleeve of Elvis's that's in a comic book style of his life from 1956. It's just a simple slip of printed paper but

the comic-panel sleeve "This is His Life" would auction off to another serious vinyl collector for $900 *without* a record. Paper condition is important. In the past, nobody really cared about sleeves: it would be like caring about CD jewel cases today. This paradox reinforces a concept in appraising: "Things that are common and tossed away today will be rare and valuable tomorrow because no one cares about them today." A sleeve of the Beatles' *Please Please Me/From Me to You* (sans record) proclaims at the top "This is the record that started Beatlemania" (Vee-Jay 581, 1964). Someone put tape on all sides and the record is history, yet if sold at auction, it'd bring $700, tape or not.

Paper ephemera is becoming huge since paper is going away and so are the days of non-computer graphic design and *real* (pre-*Photoshop*) graphic art. Graphic illustrations like those on rare record sleeves are the next big thing in collecting. In these days of banks "too big to fail," mid-century stuff might become the new money.

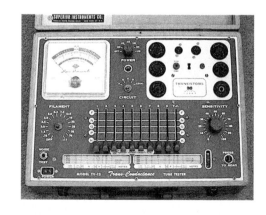

## CHRISTMAS COLLECTIBLES FOR THE DARKEST
# NIGHT

How DOES A RITUAL COME TO BE? I WILL
endeavor to prove that we're the product of history, tradition, and ritual and
that this becomes especially clear at the year's end. This case study exemplifies
how a *broad understanding of your area of interest can strengthen the depth of
your collection.*

From time immemorial, winter solstice was something to be feared and
celebrated. Across the prehistoric world, humans feared the shortest day and
endeavored to understand the darkest of all nights, wondering if they'd ever
come into light again. Think of all the collectors who are devoted to Christmas collectibles. Such an organization is the Golden Glow of Christmas Past.
This members-only, online club collects the following and more: pre-antique
Christmas ornaments, books (for children and adults), vintage Christmas music,

candy boxes, windup games, Christmas stockings and china, Christmas village houses, feather trees, garlands, Christmas Snow Babies, belsnickles and angels, snowmen, Santas, and Rudolphs—and, of course, antique nativity sets. It draws members worldwide to its annual convention, now in its 36th year.

Deep fear formed the basis of all major winter rituals, so celebrating this season led the way toward good cheer amid the cold and darkness. Let's go back a few years, actually 3,000 years, to ancient Rome. Our ancestors relied on agriculture much more than we do today. The darkest night augured that winter was at an end and spring was nigh. So all the great celebrations of winter (Christmas, the beginning of a winter festival, Hanukkah, and also Muharram, the Islamic New Year) stem from celebrations existing long before various religions and their leaders came into being.

In Rome, the celebration honored Saturn, the great god of agriculture. Because they knew spring was on its way after the long, dark winter, Romans held a month-long party. And what a party it was! Their slaves became masters and food was overflowing and their livestock were slaughtered so that animals wouldn't devour the stored grain when none was growing.

Wine was abundant at this frigid time of year when fermentation naturally ended. The entire Roman social order was turned on its ear and everyone partied hard for four weeks (and we consider a week of Christmas festivities long enough). On December 25th, the upper-class Romans also celebrated a birth, that of the god Mithra, child of the sun. It was believed Mithra was born of a rock, springing out of barrenness. And it's this theme that resonates in the Christ story, with the divine Christ born of a virgin, in a lowly manger.

Let's now look at Hanukkah which commemorates the great battle of 165 BC, when the Jews triumphed over the Hellenist (Greek) Syrians. Antiochus, the Greek king of Syria, had outlawed anything Jewish and ordered Jews to worship the Greek gods. Antiochus seized the Jews' Temple and turned it into a temple of Zeus. A number of Jews fled to the mountains under the leadership of Mattathias while others remained obedient to the Greeks.

Under Mattathias, Jews ambushed the mighty Greeks and claimed the Temple again. Judah Maccabee restored the ransacked Temple and, upon lighting the lamp, found he had enough oil for just one day. The miracle is that the menorah lasted for a full eight days. So this is the Holiday

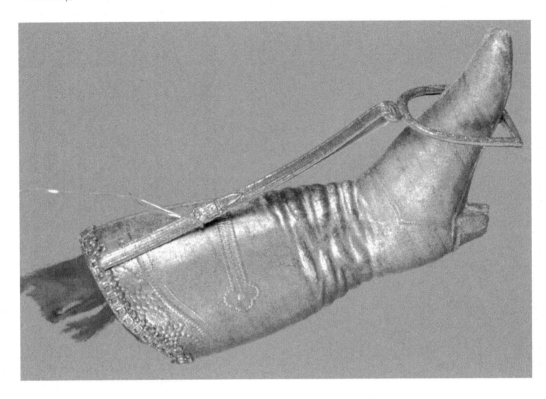

of Light, during the darkest night of the year.

Light triumphs over darkness just as it does in the spring. You see a common thread? Now enters the early Roman Christian church. The church fathers realized that the citizens were still celebrating the Saturnalia so, in the month of the winter solstice, the celebration of the infant Jesus was mixed into the celebration of rebirth.

Pope Julius in the 4th century realized it was better to switch than fight and declared Saturnalia as the Feast of the Nativity, thus absorbing pagan tradition. Actually, Egypt was the first nation to celebrate the feast and that celebration of Christmas only came to England in the 600s.

But if a drunken, pagan orgy is superimposed over a somber church celebration, the average guy might still prefer a drunken, month-long orgy. So this party went on well into the Middle Ages for more than 1,000 years. In the 13th century for example, one went to church followed by a raucous celebration that was more like Mardi Gras than Christmas. And the handsomest young man or lowliest beggar (your pick) was crowned the Lord of Misrule. The Lord of Misrule bossed everyone around for the month, and the poor

*And the handsomest young man or lowliest beggar was crowned the Lord of Misrule. The Lord of Misrule bossed everyone around for the month...*

were allowed to terrorize the homes of the rich, demanding to be fed and then watered with the best booze. As in the Saturnalia of 1,000 years previous, the lower social order happily called the tune. Believe it or not, this raucous late-medieval Christmas is one of the reasons we have a country called America.

The Puritan movement in England in the late 16th century claimed that nothing in the Bible states anything about December as a party month, nor does it state that we should all go crazy and get drunk. Thus, when Oliver Cromwell and his forces took over England in 1645, they canceled Christmas. The Pilgrim separatists who came to America in the 1620s forbad Christmas for all time (or so they thought). As the century wore on and non-Pilgrims came to these shores, the clamorous, festive holiday was again celebrated on most of the East Coast, though not in New England where Boston had outlawed it.

Christmas actually wasn't declared a federal holiday until June of 1870 and is, therefore, the newest-oldest celebration.

Around the same time of the dead winter months, Muslims will celebrate Muharram, the New Year, which also marks the death of Husayn ibn Ali, a grandson of the prophet Muhammad. Ibn Ali was killed in the battle of Karbala in AD 680. In certain Muslim countries, it is a time of mourning involving traditional chest beating rituals (its own form of commemoration).

Interestingly, royalty is also part of the common language in varied winter celebrations and, as you may recall, Christ was of the royal House of David. In some cultures the darkest night may be a time of donating food to the hungry, as a king would sustain his people. In many great religions we see echoes of a common past, which some claim to be pagan. I see it as the continuity of symbolism. The darkest night of the year, a cold and gloomy time, precedes the end of great struggle with the prospect of renewal. Spring, rebirth, and light are just around the corner.

Human history is remarkable in its transformation of traditions and this is reflected in the value of material culture associated with a ritual. To prove it, Americans will spend $465 billion this December 25th.

# DOLLS

D OLLS ARE JUST THE MOST HORRENDOUS
collectible. A client, S.G., from Rancho Cucamonga, California, sent me two
doll photographs. At first, I assumed it was a joke from my best friend who
trained as a psychiatrist and is aware of my pediophobia—a fear of humanoid-looking figures (mainly dolls). When I was a girl I screamed if I opened
a present to find another doll. So when I received these photos of ghastly
dolls (on my birthday no less) I squawked as usual. Alas, I guess I am still
learning to separate fantasy from reality. Sadly, these were no birthday joke
but a request for an appraisal from my client. This case study raises the issue
of two *aberrations found in many collections: phobia and kitsch.*

S.G. had found these horrors at a local a garage sale and asked if he had a
million dollars there. S.G. did not even have $100 there. In the 1960s, tourist
dolls were hot and those like S.G.'s little Swiss *Mädchen* were souvenirs to
torment little children upon a parent's return from abroad. The dead give-
away that S.G.'s dolls (even in pristine condition and still in their boxes)

(Evacatrin)

were made for the tourist market is that the English label reads: "Swiss Doll." But S.G. did do one thing right: he selected dolls in their original boxes. Without boxes, they'd be worth about $10 each. But with the Swiss *Mädchen* comes another kiss of death: that's the "certificate" enclosed. Ninety-nine percent of the time a paper certificate is no proof of value or authenticity. My advice to S.G. is just to keep looking because eventually he will find an amazing doll. But do not send a picture of it to me! Send it to an appraiser without pediophobia! And especially do not send me pictures of scary dolls on my birthday (though these days, I'm much more scared of birthdays than dolls).

Then the universe did it again! Another client, J.D., sent me photos of 25 to 30 dolls, quite possibly the most horrifying I've yet seen.

I chose to be brave and appraise. The backstory: J.D. called to say she'd inherited some "really ugly dolls from Spain." She needed to get rid of them because her little daughter refused to get in the car while the dolls were in the trunk (I know J.D.'s daughter is a brilliant child just by that disclosure).

What J.D. had actually inherited is approximately 30 of indeed the worst examples of the company JC

Toys Group, Dolls by Berenguer, a line by doll maker D'Anton Jos. Since the 1950s, the Berenguer family of Spain has been making these, as well as equally frightening dolls, in Castalla, Spain. This style of D'Anton Jos dolls is in "The Rotten Kids" series, circa 1970. "Rotten" because they feature terrible faces.

D'Anton Jos offers other lines of dolls in their company's vast assortment. There's "Mi Bebé" (1920s), which has a battery-operated box in the back to activate Bebé's loud wails. If you pull out the pacifier, it makes sucking noises.

Another gem is the line of "Cuchi-Cuchi" dolls: a perfect, blue-eyed, blond boy and young girl. They each display gleaming white teeth. Then there's "La Newborns": baby dolls with tiny bodies topped by sweet, angelic faces. Heinous indeed, and hyper-realistic—these are a bad dream.

Back to J.D.'s dolls: one is a tough little boy sporting a blue cap, out from under which peer eerily realistic, huge, glassy eyes. His mouth draws up in a pugnacious grimace. The next doll is a toddler girl dressed in an oversized plaid workman's shirt worn under a jean pinafore. Her knit cap sits over short, dark hair (suggesting lower class, perhaps) with lips drawn up in a pucker. Next we

*I have pediophobia, a fear of humanoid-looking figures, mainly dolls. When I was a girl I screamed if I opened a present and found a doll in a box.*

have a baby doll, a one-year old in a flowered pinafore and a bonnet. She is also doing something rather ghastly with her mouth.

And, as if we needed another reason to be depressed, J.D.'s next doll is actually sobbing. Worst of all is their vision of a five-year old girl in country-style, plaid, ethnic smock and kerchief, rudely sticking out her tongue. And the gruesome dolls go on and on.

The good news for J.D. is that these dolls have never been taken out of their original boxes nor exposed to air and dust. So if they're worth anything to a demented collector, they'll be at the top of their class.

Those dolls and toys that were never tampered with and are still in original boxes are worth far more than any with which a child has played. J.D.'s "Rotten Kids" dolls are worth $75 each.

# TOYS

A GIFT OF FRIENDSHIP IS A CAST-IRON TOY.
I had the great pleasure of preparing an estate appraisal for a talented personality native to Montecito, California, the late Jonathan Winters. This great comedian left a special toy to a wonderful friend of his (also a brilliant celebrity), the late Robin Williams. This case study *shines a light on both the value and provenance of celebrity-owned objects.*

Winters's prized gift to Williams was a Hubley Seaplane named the *Friendship*. John Hubley, founder of the 1894 company, made the only cast-iron seaplane ever manufactured by a toy company. It was modeled after the *Friendship Fokker*, the *Fokker F.VII*, originally piloted by Wilmer Stultz.

*Friendship* is an great yellow seaplane with cast-iron pontoons, arguably the best toy airplane ever made. With a series of pulleys and springs, Hubley managed to create a realistic model for a child (or adult). As the toy was pulled by a string along the ground, pulleys caused the three propellers to turn and, as it moved, the wheels turned against pontoons causing a clicker to simulate engine noise.

Hubley, maker of the *Friendship* seaplane, had studied the *Fokker,* a model from a famous aircraft manufacturer. Hubley had been a mere bank teller in Lancaster, PA, when he began making toys for his own children in his basement. Hubley fine-tuned this 13-inch toy by including a ribbed interior cabin and detailed, cast-eight piston heads in each of the three motors. Yes, three motors! In the 1920s, under the direction of the founder and director, Dutchman Anthony Fokker (the real-life Fokker), it became the best known aircraft in the world and part of this success was its design of *F.VII's* tri-motor.

My grandparents flew for the first time in a giant red *Fokker,* when it dominated the skies in the twenties and it was used as a commercial passenger aircraft in 54 countries. The toy company copied the *Fokker* following the Hubley tradition of replicating realistic forms of manufacturers. They sourced famous motorcycles, automobiles, custom characters, and architectural landmarks for cast-iron toys and banks.

Other famous aircraft which Hubley crafted into toys included

*Perfect shape would be pristine: cast-iron in perfect shape and not overpainted ... rubber tires should be original. No repairs.*

*The Lindy,* a version of Charles Lindbergh's plane, as well as *The America,* which was inspired by the tri-motor plane that Admiral Richard Byrd flew to the South Pole. *The America*

is Hubley's largest plane at 14 inches. The famous plane *Friendship* was actually modeled after Amelia Earhart's. Hubley first unveiled *Friendship* for a special party given by a famous Pittsburgh millionaire, Arthur Brown, in 1929. Brown had commissioned Hubley to make 22 yellow seaplanes, all modeled after *Friendship,* to celebrate the amazing aviatrix Amelia Earhart's achievement. Each model plane's wingspan was more than 12 inches wide, and it sported Earhart's autograph on the wings. To my knowledge, only one of these is in circulation and it was loaned to the Westmoreland Museum of American Art in Greensburg, Pennsylvania.

This celebrity's *Friendship* is not in perfect shape. Perfect shape would be pristine, untouched by children, with the original brass pull string still attached and unstretched. It would mean the original Hubley decal is still on the wing, and the cast iron in perfect shape and not overpainted. The rubber tires should be original and fresh, and the three original nickel propellers intact. No repairs anywhere would add up to "pristine condition." I have often experienced the power of an object as a receptacle of true value. But its deep worth lies in the deep sentiment of bond between these two late, great talents, as exemplified by the cast-iron toy airplane called *Friendship.*

# COUTURE

I AM A CLOTHESHORSE AND LOVE FLASHY
clothes. Vintage couture is a favorite topic so I was delighted when client
E.J. sent me a 1980s Christian Dior *Robes du Soir* ball gown, complete with
shoulder pads and 16 pounds of sequins. Eva Perón, First Lady of Argen-
tina, wore a Dior ball gown in 1950 and the dress met all the requirements
of truly amazing design: great label, fabric, and construction. The strapless
look with nipped waist and huge tulle skirt fell out of fashion until period
costume design consultants were hired to recreate the 1950s look for TV. The
nipped waist reappeared in 2013 fashion designs and Perón's gown, once an
unwanted vintage, suddenly became hot and sold for $10,000 at auction.

Great couture is hot, as this study amply illustrates. Lady Gaga sports
humongous shoulders and little else, while Nicki Minaj rocks similar shoulders.
This blast from the past is entering a modern reinvention and I predict the value
of vintage 1980s designer couture to skyrocket but *only* as "couture": defined

Left: **Dr. Elizabeth Stewart wearing Dior's** *Robes du Soir* (John Flandrick)
Right: **Heidelberg Library** (Immanuel Giel)

label CD de Christian Dior *Robes du Soir*, New York (the boutique opened in 1949). By 1950, Dior fashions made up 75% of all Paris's fashion exports and 5% of France's total export revenue! Moreover, in the 1950s, Jacques Rouet, general manager of Dior Ltd., revolutionized the world of fashion forever when he obtained a license to add Dior's name on luxury goods: ties, handbags, jewelry, and perfume.

Licensing was granted to an entire line of Dior items, but France's snooty Chamber of Commerce considered such a product line too gauche for *haute couture*. Nonetheless, profits soared and the designer label trend continues today from sunglasses to luggage.

E.J.'s gown would sell at auction today for approximately $2,000, judging by records from Skinner's Auctions and Freeman's Auctions. According to the *Daily Mail of London*, when it tracked sales at the retailer Debenhams, two-piece lady's suits with nipped waists and expanded shoulder pads are making quite a real comeback. And so is costume jewelry with those large crystal and pearl-beaded necklaces. Even ladies' pantsuits are back in again: great timing for Hillary Clinton who campaigned wearing a power pantsuit!

as an elite fashion tier of individually made and fitted garments (not the tacky, over-size, shoulder-pad gear worn with bunched-up white gym socks and athletic shoes).

E.J.'s gown is especially valuable since it's fabricated from the finest silk, hand-beaded, and displaying the

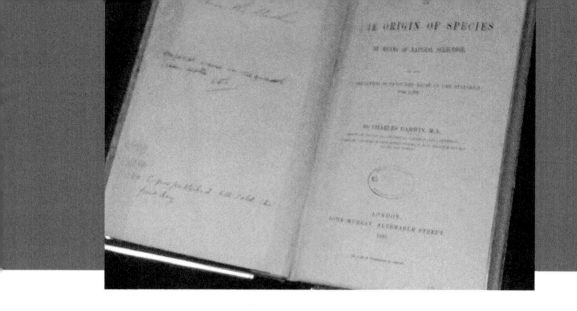

## FIRST EDITION

# BOOKS

**W**HEN A RARE FIRST EDITION OF DARWIN'S *On the Origin of Species* surfaced a few years ago, it was auctioned off for $170,569 at Christie's, London. How was it discovered? Some people store reading material in the bathroom (until cellphones, at least) and this was the custom in the bathroom of a certain English manor. The new son-in-law of this noble family was reading in the bathroom and noticed a first edition of Darwin's groundbreaking book (of which only 1,250 copies were printed in 1859) in the stack next to the loo. When the son-in-law finished, he ran to Christie's and here we have the story of a book once originally purchased for one pound and now selling for $170,000 as a rare and important piece of history. This case study illustrates *how the life of a title influences value in rare books.*

Some years ago a rare, signed book, *The Life of Brigham Young* by Tullidge, published in 1876–1880 (a first edition in which Brigham Young himself had written marginalia), was going at auction. Brigham Young had pencilled in the margins to "correct" the author and state his own ideas of his life. Young was planning for the second edition which never transpired: he died before getting corrections to the editor. Tullidge, the author, had been convinced to publicly renounce the Mormon faith because Brigham Young felt a non-Mormon author would lend more credibility and objectivity to Young's biography. Secretly, however, the author was still a practicing Mormon.

Brigham Young had also signed this biography, which is odd because the book reveals five series of his corrections. It sold for $13,225 and demonstrates how a personal, hand-notation increases a book's value if the right person scribbles in the margins!

Dr. B. sent me a photo of *The Old Mistresses' Apologue,* a letter Benjamin Franklin wrote in 1745. There are two levels of value to Dr. B.'s book, which holds a reprint of Franklin's letter. The first level is cultural: what Franklin wrote and why it wasn't published until the mid-20th century. The second is the market value of this particular book.

With regard to the cultural value issue, Franklin's advice is (and I paraphrase here):

*In all your amours you should prefer old women to young ones. You call this a paradox, and demand my reasons.*

*They are these:*
- *They know more.*
- *When they lose their looks, they endeavor to be kind.*
- *There is no hazard of children.*
- *An older woman will not spread the affair around town.*
- *In the dark all cats are gray.* (He really wrote that!)
- *Because the sin is less, since she is not a virgin.*
- *Because you won't run the risk of falling in love...and* (lastly, he adds) *they are so grateful!!*

No wonder this letter wasn't published as a book until 1926, when Mr. Phillips Russell printed it in his biography of Franklin. And in 1941, complete respectability was bestowed upon the draft when Simon & Schuster incorporated it into its *Treasury of the World's Great Letters,* delivered as a dividend to members of their Book-of-the-Month Club, a middle-brow institution offering its members various selections juried by well-respected literary critics.

Franklin's personal archive was in private hands until 1882 when the State Department purchased the lot, but this letter was not included in that transaction. The owner of the archive, Mr. Henry Stevens, held this

letter back. Stevens's widow then left it to the Chicago Historical Society, which also did not care for it and sold the draft to the brothers Phillip and A.S. Rosenbach. In 1938, the original was exhibited at Philadelphia Free Library.

So was the witty Mr. Franklin also a rake? There is some material proof: his wife bore him three children but he did father a child out of wedlock who, amazingly, was raised in Franklin's home. And there exists further evidence of rakishness in the book *Road to Revolution: Benjamin Franklin in England, 1765–1775,* in which author C. Currey describes Franklin's friendship with a Sir Francis Dashwood (aka Lord Le Despencer), the postmaster of England at the time when Franklin was postmaster of the colonies.

Despencer had an influential (and very kinky) gentleman's club called Medmenham Monks, or as some called it, the Hellfire Club, in Buckinghamshire.

Ironically, it was a former Cistercian abbey, and Despencer redesigned it from its original 1145 state into a lurid garden of lust. The grounds featured pornographic statues and inscriptions with indecent artwork echoing erotic Roman frescoes and portraits of famous historic courtesans. Currey quotes Franklin: "The design is whimsical and puzzling in its imagery, [and] is as evident below the earth as above it." This secret society was mainly composed of very powerful men selected by Despencer. Among those 70 men was Franklin.

The men were labeled "monks" and, unsurprisingly, the women, "nuns." In 1765, Franklin became a club member and mingled with other "monks" and "nuns" in an elaborately decorated cave. Franklin wrote that he met such prominent "nuns" as Lady Mary Wortley Montagu, as well as notable "monks" such as Frederick, Prince of Wales.

Now to the second value of Dr. B.'s book. Although only 2,000 such books were printed, primarily due to the scandalous nature of the letter, many other unauthorized printings were done over the years. So Dr. B.'s book, in perfect condition, is worth only $40. But Franklin's suggestion to take an older mistress (to the mind of this mature, single appraiser) is worth gold!

Französische Generäle. (1799—1800.)

Mitglieder der Commune. (1793—1794.)

chener Bilderbogen.

Nro. 800.

Herausgegeben und verlegt von Braun & Schneider in

# BOOKS

WHEN TO SLASH AND WHEN TO SAVE: a client called to ask if she'd be ruining an old book by excising its color plates. She said, "They are perfect for framing in my home." This case study considers *color plates, and a bit about print history so you can decide what the illustrations, as compared with an intact book, may be worth.*

All the book illustrations up until the 1840s (especially if colored) were etched first on copper or metal plates, though occasionally wood was used. The prints were first hand-colored and then placed inside the book which was termed "tipping in." All of it was done by hand, and no machines were used. This slow and careful process should be treasured: after 1840 a new technology for printing was invented, which was termed chromolithography, and book production was mechanized.

How does one spot chromolithography? The colors are bright and gaudy and the coloration used paints, gums, and acids, which were applied to flat stones or metal plates and then transferred to paper. After 1900, commercial printing became completely mechanized, so that plates in the book are one and the same with the page paper.

Another clue to an early illustration plate is the use of fine, little tissue covers. What were those used for? They protected the ink from any contact with a printed page when the book was closed, and from rubbing against the opposite page, which was mainly rough-textured wood pulp.

Sometimes you'll find illustration pages which are printed on glossy, sturdy, but finer, paper than the ordinary printed page. That is an indication of age, because the artwork may have been tipped in by hand, and that is rarely done today. Some fine, expensive, limited-edition, collector volumes still use this technique.

In some such books, you'll see a print that has been cut separately, mounted on heavier stock, and only then inserted in the book. This is to give the effect of framing inside the book. You can tell if you have a reprint of a book post-1900 if the publication date is 1840, yet the prints are photo-mechanical. How can you spot this? Get out a magnifying glass and look to see if you spy little *dots*. Then you know it's the dot-matrix pattern of inking in use today.

So now to my client's question: should she get out the razor blade to make single pictures or preserve the book intact? The key is really the condition of the book. Condition dictates value: only if the book is in poor condition should you even think about slicing out plates. What follows is a short lesson on how to judge condition.

Follow the bibliophile's gradated stages. "Fine condition" means the book looks brand-new, with its original dust jacket. If it never had a dust jacket, the cover (usually made with cloth) must be in perfect shape. The earliest known flap style of a (modern) dust jacket was used after 1850. If the book is in fine condition, then it will have pert edges and corners.

Next, a book in "very good condition" is practically perfect. It may have a slight corner crush, but to the average person the book will look great. A very good condition book will not have its price cut away from the dust jacket as missing prices jettsion value. Also, a very good condition book will never be a second edition with an updated dust cover.

There are two categories in which I would allow someone to take prints from an antique book. A book in

Some fine, expensive, limited edition collectors' books still use this technique called "tipping in."

"good condition" retains its original dust jacket and appears as lightly read. The standard good condition book (unless the book is incredibly rare) is not being collected so the illustrations may be removed.

Then there are the books in "fair condition" which will never be of much value. Like mine: I toss dust jackets, actually read the book, and also dog-ear pages. In fact, I write conversations with the author in the book. Value is based on condition and not much else, except extreme rarity.

Therefore, if the old books are in the lower two categories, I give my blessing to remove the plates. But be sure to use a special razor edge meant for this. If you really love the book in its entirety and it's not in good shape, there are special artisans who restore and rebind old books. But this is so rare and specialized a service that you'll pay quite a bit. I did a search in my area for valuable antique and book restoration but couldn't locate a single local artisan.

Once those illustrations are out of a book, are they worth anything? The answer is yes, possibly. One plate from McKenney's *History of the Indian Tribes of North America* which features upwards of 20 plates, might sell if the plate is actually

Library, Alexandria, Egypt *(RedTurtle)*

near-perfect. They've been selling for $500 or so. If that book is in fine condition, then the whole thing will still sell for up to $100,000. So unless an old book is truly on its last legs, it is not worth dissection.

Finally, we know something in our world is valuable if it gets stolen. Miles Harvey's *The Island of Lost Maps: A True Story of Cartographic Crime* documents the real saga of the worst book thief in history who stole countless map illustrations. Gilbert Joseph Bland Jr. was a strange recluse who slashed and dashed his way through the world's great libraries until he was finally caught in 1995.

Prints in a book can be valuable and are generally more prized if left unmolested inside your book, rather than mounted on a wall.

## ANIMAL SKINS & SECRETS OF THE KNIGHTS

# TEMPLAR

THIS IS A PARTICULARLY CURIOUS STORY told through B.B., a great lady's daughter. The mother of B.B. taught at the University of California until well into her nineties. She took her students under her wing and was known to many as "Grandmother." When the students returned home to various countries they sent Grandmother special gifts from their countries. This story is about the gift of an old letter, and this case study instructs in *my own personal research techniques. Research is so often the real key to unlocking an object's value.*

B.B. knows two things about this gift. Someone thought it was valuable enough to collect and assign a call letter within a library. She wrote it might be as old as the 1700s since the type of parchment dates from that era. At the time when parchment was in use, historians estimate that less than 30% of the populace were literate, so perhaps clergy or nobility were meant to read it. B.B. brought this parchment document to my office, and after I examined it firsthand, the research began. I had an inkling this could be something special, but how special exactly? It turns out that it's scholarship worthy: a faint date of what I think is 1307 appears at the very top of the parchment and at bottom is the faint signature "Philip." I did a search of notable 1307 historic events to try to find a connection between the date and name—a lot was going on in 1307! For example, William Tell shot an apple off his son's head and Albrecht the First made his son King of Bohemia. Then Cousin Henrik took over as King of Bohemia. None of those seem to fit. This event did however: in October of 1307 French King Philip IV convicted and jailed the Knights Templars. And so I continued researching.

In 1120, eight Christian knights who had been ordained in the Latin Kingdom of Jerusalem were charged with the protection of pilgrims as they traveled to and from Jerusalem. The Templars grew from a secret society and followed the Rule of the Order: obedience, poverty, and chastity. That did not preclude battling, and the Order fought on the side of big money —those who paid for protection during the Crusades. They fought for the Holy Land against the followers of Muhammad, but, in essence, they were mercenaries

who were paid to defend kings and nobles. They enjoyed perks, such as exemptions from certain rules, taxes, and, as Pope Clement V of Avignon claimed, moral behavior. The Knights had more money and influence than even the French king, and by 1307 they were generally envied and loathed.

To make a long and complex history short, the Knights loaned French King Philip heaps of money. But the Paris capitol revolted against Philip: he was a profligate spender, and bread for the common people was very scarce. Yet, the Templars continued to defend Philip. The pope is said to have written a letter to Philip in 1307, asking for Philip's permission to investigate the Templars. But Philip was crafty—and did I also mention he was in their debt? So, without the pope's permission, Philip acted in stealth and hastened to seize as many Knights as he could and throw them into prison.

In 1307, Pope Clement V's Vatican ordered letters be written to all bailiffs of the kingdoms of France, England, Iberia, Germany, Italy, and Cyprus, requesting that representatives of these countries arrest and torture these Templars under the command of Phillip. Also in 1307, the pope jumped on the bandwagon of the Inquisition and two main leaders of the Templars were forced to "confess" and (not so mysteriously) were burned. As many as 100 Knights confessed thereafter, 54 of whom were burned at the stake in Paris in 1310. Then in 1314, the Order was virtually driven completely underground as two of the top leaders of the Knights were burned at the stake. Could this gift from a student to Grandmother actually be one of the letters from King Philip directing officials to capture the Templars?

Historical documents relating to the Templars are still turning up today and a famous example is a *Chinon Parchment*, discovered in 2001 in the Vatican Secret Archive. The existence of this document had truly always been assumed, since it had been referred to in other documents long before it was discovered. Previous to the finding of this *Chinon Parchment*, medieval historians had studied letters between Philip and the pope and determined that this document might exist, as well as another, perhaps written thereafter. Historians believe someone will find this missing link in the story of the demise of the Knights.

Barbara Frale, the historian who discovered the *Chinon* document in 2001, is an Italian paleographer at the Vatican Secret Archives and

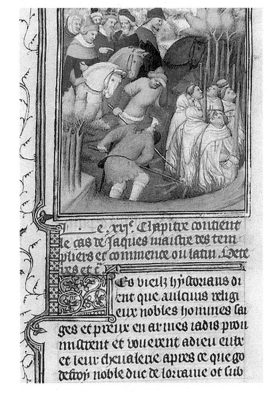

surmises someone will eventually find other documents dealing with charges of the Templars' secret initiation practices. Though Grandmother's document may not be the missing link, it turns out B.B.'s parchment is important. I was invited to bring B.B. to a meeting with two eminent UCSB scholars: a professor of medieval Italian languages and his wife, a scholar of medieval literature. The document's owner was quite impressed with their interest, and donated it to UCSB's Medieval Studies Department for their research into a connection with France's King Philip IV ("the Fair"). My research paid off, so remain persistent in digging out an object's true story.

Funerary dress, King Pakal of Palenque, 7th c. *(Wolfgang Sauber)*

## JEWELRY, SILVER, METAL, AND
# STONE

H ERE'S A TALE OF REAL SKULDUGGERY:
A thriller-detective-blackmarket story centering on the world of ancient artifacts. This case study exemplifes *the pitfalls of cultural property*. The U.S. State Department's Bureau of Educational and Cultural Affairs has a team called the Cultural Property Advisory Committee. It consists of 11 private citizens, appointed by the President and comprised of various experts in the fields of archaeology and anthropology, in the international sale of cultural property, and in the representation of museums' interests. It was made possible by the 1970 UNESCO Convention, which passed an act allowing any of the convention signatories to submit requests to the U.S. seeking to control imports of certain archaeological or anthropological artifacts.

Presently, the U.S. has cultural property agreements with, and has taken emergency State Department measures to protect certain imports from, Bolivia,

Cambodia, Columbia, Cyprus, El Salvador, Guatemala, Honduras, Italy, Mali, Nicaragua, Peru, and, as of a few years ago, China. On its website (culturalheritage.state.gov), the Cultural Heritage Center provides illustrated charts of items that should not be exported and notes their dates of restriction. If one can prove an artifact left the country of origin prior to the dates the restrictions went into effect, one is on safe ground when considering its purchase. The act is meant to protect against pillage which, as we saw with museums in Iraq, is of critical international concern. I find it amusing to picture a squad of trained PhD SWAT archaeologists (they exist)!

In the case of the Classic Mayan stone tools sent to me by B.F. for an appraisal, it was deemed illegal to export them after 1991. According to my research, this collection comes from Guatemala and is called "eccentric form" stone tools from the lowland Mayan culture. They weren't used as weapons, but rather as ceremonial objects, and are 10 to 25 cm in length, crafted from flint or obsidian to form crescents, stars, and notched points (unusual shapes). In 1991, the Ministry of Culture & Sports in Guatemala asked the U.S. State Department to help control such exports. If my client

purchased these in Guatemala and exported them to the U.S. after 1991, the collection would have no market value. He needs proof of this in the form of an export certificate.

Even if the artifact is imported from a country that is not its country of origin, an export certificate from the country of origin must be produced. This is to protect a country's national patrimony. If an object has been stolen, it may not enter the U.S., and title or ownership to an object cannot be conveyed. Thus, an illegally imported article has *no* value.

If a pillaged item is sent abroad— whether it's discovered above or below ground—it's still considered an illicitly exported cultural artifact. The U.S. Customs Service or the FBI may recover archaeological and anthropological objects which have entered the U.S. illegally. Two registries I use list art and artifacts that have been reported as stolen. The Getty Museum pioneered Object ID, which is the minimal level of documentation necessary to identify an object. To see how seriously this issue is taken, go to one of these websites: the Art Loss Register (based in NY), London's ICOM Red List (based in Paris), or Interpol (based in Lyon, France). Anything Italian that's highly prized is specialized, and so

(Awilix)

the Italian Art Police are a special and separate branch of law enforcement. Called the Comando Carabinieri, they're a crack team of police and art and antique (as well as anthropologic) experts. Amazingly, they're trained in hand-to-hand combat! France also has their specialized art police: the Office Central de Lutte, or the Office for the Fight.

Classic Mayan artifacts are very, very rare and have led to deep plots involving the FBI and art police. A recent discovery entitled "Straight Outta Brooklyn" (*Archaeology Magazine*), was that of a 500 pound carved-stone Mayan jaguar head from Guatemala. It was finally discovered in a Brooklyn garage and the Brooklyn police ended up apprehending a jaguar head. This major discovery both intrigued and puzzled the men in blue. Where would they put the handcuffs?

To make matters worse, the jaguar head was a sacrificial ceremonial item. Can you picture a man caught in the jaws of a vicious jaguar, arms outstretched, screaming in agony? When Fernando Paniagua, Director of Guatemala's Registry of Cultural Assets, was contacted with the astounding news that the head had been found, he admitted he'd never heard of it. The story ends well, highlighting both the

kindness of fate and the fact that these Brooklyn police were also trained art historians. The exotic jaguar head is now in the Museum of Archaeology and Ethnology in Guatemala City.

On a related note, I refer you to three U.S. federal laws:

- *The Archaeological Resources Protection Act*
- *The Native American Graves and Repatriation Act*
- *The Abandoned Shipwreck Act*

Lastly, for an appraiser, if an item is illegal it has *no* value since it can't legally be sold. So do check that Cultural Heritage Center's site before the art police meet up with you upon returning from abroad with ancient treasure.

## LOOTING OF ANTIQUITIES
# TODAY

J UNE IS ANCIENT ANTIQUITIES MONTH AT
all major auction houses. I love classic militaria. In fact, I have several collections (immense sabres, military dress coats, war medals) and am always
on the alert for things regimental. I attended Christie's Antiquities sale
in New York to watch the battle over an old Greek bronze helmet (circa
650–620 BC). It's adorned with a frightening curled spike on the crest, and
features incised mythological scenes surrrounding the crown. The auction's
estimate was $350,000 to $550,000 and the helmet, almost 2,600 years old,
is in perfect condition! This auction also featured an Egyptian diorite portrait
head (circa 380–340 BC), in the tradition of ancient Egyptian sculptors who
portrayed subjects as eternally youthful and beautiful. Its estimated value was
$500,000 to $700,000. There's big money in antiquities because they'll never
be seen again. This case study continues with *the perils of collecting antiquities
and how to investigate ownership.*

Looting antiquities is a major issue in Greece, where in some cities, such as Athens, treasures can be found only inches below soil. Dozens of illegally exported finds have been returned to Greece over the past few years, including four masterpieces from Los Angeles's J. Paul Getty Museum.

Ancient Egyptian treasures were recently found near Alexandria's harbor. A seven-foot-four-inch, nine-ton pylon, was discovered from the palace of Queen Cleopatra of the Ptolemaic dynasty. It had supported a temple of Isis, the pharaonic goddess of fertility and magic, and apparently toppled into the sea during a 4th century AD earthquake. "Magic" because it's possible that in 1 BC, the palace temple might've housed Queen Cleopatra while she wooed Roman general Marc Antony (before both committed suicide following their defeat by Augustus Caesar).

When the earthquake hit the palace in the 4th century, its stunning force scattered 20,000 ancient Egyptian artifacts throughout the sea off Alexandria's coast. Before the Arab Spring and subsequent upheaval in Egypt, the excavators had discovered dozens of ancient sphinxes along with remnants of a very old Alexandrian lighthouse, considered in ancient times to be one of the Seven Wonders of the World. Alexandria, founded by Alexander the Great in 331 BC, was also the site of the Alexandrian Library. In 2008, UNESCO and Egypt unveiled great plans to build a $140 million museum with a submarine on rails for visitors to view Cleopatra's sunken city. The project proposed to lead tourists through several underwater tunnels of the museum as early as 2011 but, as of 2015, I'd found nothing on UNESCO's website about such a museum. Since 2015 inaugurated a horrid year of archaeological terrorism, it may be just as well.

The next major hurdle for the archaeological market may be that of stolen objects—a shame as these are our common ancestry. Collectors should be aware that current political situations may lead to major ownership issues in the future. Buyer beware and check artlossregistry.com!

## HOW TO DATE A "MADE-IN"

# ANTIQUE

Mʏ CLIENT C.W. SENT ME PHOTOS OF a few antiques to price and for which I heartily endeavored to find her a moneymaker. C.W.'s batch included only one item of interest, a brass tray 38 inches in diameter. The back read "Made in Hong Kong." The phrase "Made in" is important since we use that stamped mark as a dating tool. Before 1890, imports into the U.S. were not required to have any marks. It's hard to imagine for us now, when every label states a manufacturer and place of origin. Today, the country of origin is a marketing tool and logos as trademarks are recognized worldwide. This case study instructs in ascertaining *an object's date by understanding import-export laws and "country of origin" marks.*

In 1914, Congress passed a law requiring the phrase "Made in ___," written in English and with the country of origin legible to Americans. The exception was the Japanese, who insisted their wares be stamped with the name of their country "Ni-Pon," as they called it. They used the stamp "NIPPON" until 1921 (the year of the Washington Naval Conference, which limited

Japanese naval power), when the U.S. Customs officials required all Japanese wares to be marked "Japan." After 1945, the U.S. required "Made in Japan," and then "Made in Occupied Japan" until 1952 (when Japan was no longer occupied), as termed by the Allied Forces.

By the end of WWI and WWII, the world realized a host of new borders. The use of the mark "Czecho-Slovakia" will easily date an import from the 1920s. Through all these border shifts, the German glass industry was finally moved to Poland in the 1950s. From 1945 to 1950, German imports were often marked "U.S. Zone." By the late 1940s, when East and West Germany separated, items were often marked "West Germany," and then "Western Germany."

Back to C.W.'s brass tray. In the world of Asian imports, this tells quite a story of material culture. When I was a child, and something read "Made in Japan," it implied it was a cheap, plastic gewgaw due to Japanese low production and labor costs after the war. Then Japan changed and "Made in Japan" meant quality. Taiwan (then Hong Kong) took over the cheap gewgaw market, but soon things changed for the better. From 1949 to the mid-1970s, the U.S. had no trade with mainland China. When you see "Made in the Republic of China," or "Made in R.O.C.," it indicates the wares are from Taiwan. The rare Chinese wares we received were marked "Made in the People's Republic of China" until the late 1970s. Indonesia came into existence in 1949, and Malaysia in 1963, so items marked with those names are recent.

"Made in China" porcelain is often from 1970 or later. But here's the kicker: the Chinese invented porcelain but they also invented the art of the fake. This wasn't always intended to deceive; it was to honor a potter and alongside that went fake markings. Two markings are indicative of later copies: one is a rubber stamp "China" and the other is a rubber stamp chop mark (character) under the glaze. These marks are primarily red, but if blue, they're usually older.

Because of the McKinley Tariff Act, marks on Asian wares displaying Western characters did not occur before the 1890s. So we can date this tray to the 1970s from its "Made in Hong Kong" marking. It's not an antique (an object dating back 100 years or more), but it is very large. These big brass trays became 1970s coffee tables on foldable legs. With legs, its value is about $350.

## HERE LIE THE BONES OF CROMWELL:

# CARVINGS

O LIVER CROMWELL'S HEAD WAS FOUND in March, 1960, after 301 years, and was sent to its final resting place in a cemetery at Cambridge College. The rest of his body was never located. Cromwell, the 17th-century Lord Protector of England, Scotland, and Ireland from 1653 to 1658, died of natural causes (albeit disgraced) in 1658. When my client A.T. sent a photo of his wife's antique, English-carved, wooden plaque, I remembered the cult of Cromwell of the 19th century. In a worship of all things medieval, Cromwell was deemed a heroic rebel and the Britons of that era made a sport of searching for his bones. This is nationalism at its best. This case study exemplifies the *imperative of a good understanding of history in researching valuable antiques of unknown age.*

The plaque was engraved with the initials "O.C." Of course, as always, I started from an intuition: "O.C." could refer to Oliver Cromwell. Cromwell's entire body (including head) had been buried at Westminster Abbey in 1658. After the Restoration of the English monarchy in 1660, Cromwell was such a hated figure that the English dug his three-years-dead body out of Westminster Abbey's lead-lined vaults and tried him in court for war crimes. His corpse, unable to defend itself, was found guilty of regicide and strung up on the gallows. Since he was already dead, this didn't faze him, so the English took him down and decapitated him. His head, after a colorful and macabre history, now resides in Cambridge, but what of the rest of his bones?

A.T.'s wooden plaque tells part of the story. A small box on the wooden plaque is also engraved with the initials O.C. In the 19th century, a few of Cromwell's actual bones were discovered scattered from London to Yorkshire, and so the cult of Cromwell grew. It was thought more bones were discoverable and the English public seemed to find them everywhere. The Victorian fascination with the death of great white men, ghosts, murder, and all things funereal gave rise to a Cromwellian cult of relics and plaques like A.T.'s. Those British parlors also needed repositories for the bones one found. The hanging fruitwood plaque

depicts a framed cartouche of foliate leaves and four flying putti circling around a tiny, round, hinged box (bone holder). The box is carved with a laurel and feather garland around the intertwined initials of O.C. Supporting the wreath is a heraldic shield showing the Cross of St. George (England), the Saltire Cross of St. Andrew (Scotland), and the Stringed Harp (Ireland), centered by the Lion Rampant (London). The motto beneath the guilloche (carved as a ribbon) is *pax quaeritur bello*: "Peace is sought by war."

The heraldic shield is almost identical to those of the original Cromwellian coat of arms and the motto is definitely his. What is not 17th century is the style: flowery, overblown, ornate, and religious. Cromwell wouldn't have decorated plaques with such delicate angels; he was not a sentimental man. He was a political animal and a decidedly non-religious one. He got down to business and signed Charles I's death warrant—after which Charles was soon beheaded in 1649. The design elements on this plaque are not Cromwellian, but rather of the 19th century.

Cromwell overthrew the Stuart monarchy of Charles I because he hated the vanity and sensuality of the

High Church of England, the church of Charles I.

Oliver Cromwell was the only non-royal to sit on England's throne and his rigid, austere aesthetic influenced everything. This included 17th-century decorative arts, as well as the military uniforms of the 180,000 dead in two English civil wars.

Pre-Cromwell England had been torn apart by religious strife. The factions included the Calvinists, the Laudianists, the Arminianists, the High Church and, perhaps most important for Americans, those most stringent Puritans who claimed their tenets were the only route to God. Cromwell was most likely a closet Puritan, bent on doing away with anything religious or visually frivolous. His favorite chair was plain, spartan, straight-backed, and armless—just square oak and leather.

He would never have countenanced a plaque of winged cherubs surrounding his initials. Why then did the plaque's 19th-century creator go to such lengths to get the historicism right and not the style?

Actually, the period of mid-19th-century England had no original style of its own: neither in art, furniture, clothing, nor architecture. If a society fears a fast-moving present, its psychology is to bury its head in the past. And Britain did just that stylistically for 50 years, as none of their decorative arts embodied a distinct style.

Add to that the Victorian era's sexual repression and it's not surprising the era sparked a cultural fascination with sex and its cousin death. This carved plaque is therefore a 19th-century fantasy of cult-figure worship and worth $500, not $5,000 (as it would be if it were actually 17th century).

## HOW TO FIND PROVENANCE: A STERLING

# SECRET

A TENTATIVE VOICE PHONED AND SAID "I have a brown dresser with knobs." It's not an uncommon occurence. Usually the next sentence is: "So what's it worth?" Despite the plethora of uneventful calls, I sometimes discover a fascinating story and what follows is just this type of big find. This case study reveals how I go about searching for clues in an effort to *attach an object to its original owner, and how that impacts its value.*

I received the call from a well-spoken, older lady in San Francisco. She asked to meet at her deceased mother's ranch outside Paso Robles, in the middle of nowhere. The old farmhouse, boarded up and abandoned for 20 years, was cold and dusty but my client was raised in this structure: a basic farmhouse with concrete floors. There was much acreage so another house had been built on the back forty for her parents, and I toured that deserted, boarded-up house as well. My client needed an estate appraisal because the land, houses, and personal property were to be split among heirs. In the parents' house I was arrested by a beautiful portrait of a lovely young woman with blue flowers circling her black hair. It was on the living room wall, dated 1853, and initialed "E. von L.," but unsigned. My client explained this was her great-great-great-grandmother and a relation to one of the kings of Prussia (or that was family lore).

Back in Santa Barbara, I researched the items' provenance. Often in tracking provenance, an appraiser first attempts a best-case scenario and then drills down to see if the the evidence is there to support that. What if these items had been used in the court of Frederick the Great in the 18th century? I knew that Frederick the Great had a son Augustus who grew to be a great general and led the Germans against Napoléon in the Battle of Leipzig. I've seen the famous war monument in Leipzig, as it's actually my own grandfather's hometown. Augustus had a wife, but no children. However, I knew how some royal men lived, and searched for another possible family. Indeed, Augustus did have

a mistress, whom he had made his beloved countess.

In 1850, he'd presented his mistress with a mansion in Poland, a long way from his noble wife. His mistress bore him five children, all of whom lived in the mansion. According to my genealogy site, one of those children was a young woman in her early twenties with the initials matching those in the portrait: "E. von L." I judge from the portrait's clothing that she was from that same time period. Provenance works by unraveling puzzles, so I looked again at a silver dresser mirror and I saw that it was stamped "Hossgauer," firmly establishing it as a Johann George Hossgauer piece. He was a late 18th-century Berlin artist, designer, and architect.

The only other silver pieces that I was able to trace to Hossgauer are in the collection of the Queen of England! If you recall your royalty, Queen Victoria married Prince Albert, who was Prussian (Hohenzollern) royalty. Now I was onto something! Hossgauer was a particular favorite of Frederick the Great, who'd requested Hossgauer design a small building at his main residence, *Sanssouci,* to house his sizeable art collection.

Finally, I researched how Prussian royalty managed to end up in a

Frederick the Great's *Sanssouci:* palace and park, Potsdam, Germany *(Suse)*

distant farm in early California. E. von L. had married a count, and then died in childbirth. But her son lived, grew up, and moved to the U.S. in the late 19th century after meeting a lady from the American South. I drew a blank until I found someone in the son's family tree who had died in California. So the link was made and my client really was the great-great-great-great-granddaughter of Frederick the Great of Prussia! Quite a ways from a Prussian palace to a Paso Robles cattle ranch.

The silver tea set and mirror had been crafted by Frederick's silver artist for the royal court. I informed my client of her Hohenzollern ancestry, and that she was also related to other dignitaries such as the Queen Mother and Queen Elizabeth, as well as Nicholas and Alexandra of Russia (Nicholas was a cousin of the House of Windsor). My client commented "That's why as children we ate with sterling silver that was monogrammed with a double eagle!"

Certain stories of royal provenance disappear over many generations. Not much had been known about E. von L., since she died at 27 after giving birth (which may have also been hushed up since the child was illegitimate). The value of the royal silver ranged in the hundreds of thousands of dollars.

## THE TRIUMPH OF LOVE:

# JEWELRY

I WAS SENT A LOVELY 18-KARAT GOLD AND enamel diamond pin in the shape of a 2.5-inch mandolin. My client had inherited this treasure encased in a fine red Cartier box. Aunt Kigi had been quite a lady and men had showered her with jewels. Although many jewelers made musically themed trinkets, my client had always assumed this was Cartier, and indeed Cartier jewels were Kigi's favorite. This case points out the *dangers of presuming connections between and object and its container or environment*.

I searched for any Cartier attempts at fashioning tiny jeweled instruments, but couldn't find such a brooch. I looked into the design number on the red box (C914) and found the *C* line of Cartier's did not include brooches. Further, the trademark *Les Must de Cartier* dates from 1972, when a group of investors bought the family-run Cartier, that began in 1847. The new owners

Above: Pierre Cartier, brother of Jacques and Louie, with wife and daughter, 1926
Left: Cartier Building in Lisbon *(Elfabso)*

introduced a more modern-looking line and, according to the $400 red leather book *Les Must de Cartier* that Assouline published in 2003, the early years of *Les Must* "were a time when it was in good taste to trample underfoot the values of yesterday." The book goes on to say that luxury was not dead, it just needed to be reinvented, and Cartier justified luxury by offering it as a more perfect form of modernity. No, I told my client, Kigi's brooch was certainly not a Cartier. The key to an object is always the object itself, not the box, frame, or setting. Some of the finest pieces are found completely out of context.

This brooch was actually classical and much older and finer than the box it was found in. It harkened back to a tradition beginning with the Greek vase painting of Apollo and his lute. I found no Cartier maker's stamp and no eagle hallmark—the French hallmark for 18-karat or 750 gold. By the way, 750 means the brooch was

750% gold, out of a total of 1000% and the other 250% includes various reinforcing metals. So I suspect Aunt Kigi put this brooch into one of the many Cartier boxes she may have had lying around. This in no way takes away from this brooch's rarity, beauty, and value. Though small, it's realistic and the proportions are very accurate. Great quality is evident in the workmanship of the strings, with each separately strung. The exquisite tailpiece is white gold with diamonds and is also hinged. The headstock contains eight separate tuning pegs and the fingerboard is black and ebonized. All around the sound hole there's a black and gold-chased (incised) leaf design. Solid 18-karat gold creates a chased pick guard, and the back is enameled with alternate colors as in the Italian "melon" style.

I believe this piece dates from the first quarter of the 20th century and could have been custom-made for Aunt Kigi. The closest comparable brooch is valued at $8,000.

# OBJECTS OF
# CURIOSITY

IMAGINE WHAT A YOUNG RECEPTIONIST at the museum must have thought when she caught sight of ancient fingers (horrible and creeping upwards of 400 years). A visitor to the museum, who remains anonymous, believed them to be the true relics of the amazing astronomer Galileo. You may be wondering how the museum director determined the two fingers were indeed Galileo's, aside from a 1905 description of the jar. Apparently, the museum *already* had one of Galileo's fingers in its possession and the DNA from that digit determined that the other two fingers must also be Galileo's. In a singular twist of fate, Galileo's third finger had been on display at the museum for quite some time. The next two case studies demonstrate just how *wide-ranging and eclectic collections can be, and how obsessive some collectors become.*

If you remember your science, Galileo was ordered to stand trial before the Inquisition for heresy in 1633, and he was found guilty. Guilty, because in his book *Dialogue Concerning the Two Chief World Systems,* published 1632, he wrote that the sun was motionless at the center of the universe, and that the earth revolved around it. He claimed the earth was not at the center, where the church had always insisted God placed it. The Inquisitors declared his claim blasphemous and Galileo was ordered to curse his book. When he didn't, he was promptly imprisoned and his book banned, as were all books he'd written or was ever to write.

It's fascinating that the museum had possession of Galileo's third finger, the one we all raise in salute to things we consider incredulous and scornful (especially, of course, when driving). And one wonders by just what method the museum chose to display that third finger pointing at the viewer. Galileo's opinion of the Inquisition's findings is on display today in Florence.

The museum displays the two new fingers along with his third, in a less offensive salute. All in a stately room, of course. How did the fingers get away? After his death, Galileo was moved in 1737 to a final resting place at Italy's Cathedral of Santa Croce and that's when someone supposedly cut off his fingers and removed all his teeth. The missing fingers were unnoticed until 1905.

The custom of cutting body parts off corpses, especially those of some stature, was not uncommon. St. Fermin of Amiens, the patron saint of Pamplona, is associated with the running of the bulls but it was really the 4th-century Bishop of Toulouse who converted St. Fermin to Christianity. Pieces of him are on display. And it was actually the French St. Saturninus who met with locals' displeasure and was tied to bulls' feet and dragged to his death. For some reason, St. Fermin was conflated with his converter and now he's the Saint of the Running of the Bulls.

Stranger still, is that Toulouse's cathedral, Notre Dame du Tour (Our Lady of the Bulls), is where, as legend has it, the bulls stopped running with poor St. Saturninus in 257 AD. This cathedral was formerly a temple site for worship of the sacred bull!

Frequently in art history, paganism and Christianity are intertwined. Amiens's cathedral houses some of St. Fermin's body parts and his martyrdom is duly venerated in 16th-century priceless plaques which graphically detail all his history: decapitation, grave site discovery, and exhumation of his body.

St. Bernadette of Lourdes, though not 400 years old, has been dead quite a while and on view in a glass coffin at the Church of St. Gildard in Nevers, France, since 1925.

# BLOOD

SOMEONE GRABBED THESE TREASURES before us: a boxed piece of royal wedding cake from the marriage of Prince William and Kate Middleton. The slice and box were auctioned in December, 2014, in Beverly Hills for $6,000. The Buckingham Palace reception featured 649 other boxes of traditional wedding fruitcake for friends and family and each tin box contained a printed card from the Prince of Wales and Duchess of Cornwall. The box measured 5½ by 4¼ by 2 inches and was designed by Peter Windett and Sally Mangum. The cake itself was baked by Fiona Cairns for the April, 2011, wedding. $6,000 for a piece of very old cake! Gee Chang, the female CEO of an online marketplace called listia.com, purchased the piece of cake to donate it, in a gesture intended to convey that all collectors should have the opportunity to own cake (as in "Let them eat cake!").

What follows is another strange case study highlighting *how irrationally the*

*public reacts to celebrity objects.* Operating online from its base on Guernsey in the UK Channel Islands, PFC Auctions attempted to sell a vial of Ronald Reagan's blood in 2012. Yes, you read right. But PFC was forced to withdraw Ronnie's blood under pressure from the Reagan Presidential Foundation. The story, as told on PFC Auctions' website, is truly wild. President Reagan was shot by John Hinckley Jr. in March, 1981, just as he was leaving the Washington Hilton Hotel following an address to a group of union officials. Reagan was rushed to George Washington University Hospital. The vial of blood which the auction house offered was labeled with the president's age (70), referring physician's name (Aaron), name of the Director of Laboratory Medicine at George Washington University Hospital (Marsh), and instructions to Dr. Marsh to test for lead levels in the blood. A printed instruction form for the lab accompanied this vial of prestigious blood.

The consigner, who had remained anonymous throughout all this hoopla, offered a strange story of the vial's origins. He reportedly had purchased it through a public auction in February of 2012 for $3,500. I researched a bit further and found provenance in the form of the consigner's own personal statement on that auction house website. He claimed his mother obtained the vial in the early 1980s while working in the lab which tested Reagan's blood. Amazingly, the mother's boss allowed her to take the vial home in April, 1981.

And here's where the story reads like a spy thriller. The consigner wrote that before he decided to let PFC auction the vial, he called the Reagan National Library and spoke to an unnamed head librarian, whom he claimed was a federal agent. That agent didn't want to purchase the vial; rather, he wanted the owner to donate it, but the owner refused.

According to the consigner's full report, the agent said over the phone, "Don't move from your house for about 30 minutes while I call the FBI." The owner replied, "Am I in any kind of trouble? Will there be some black cars, SUVs, and helicopters hovering over my home?" The FBI librarian replied, "Not yet, but possibly in the very near future." Apparently, it depended upon what the FBI "librarian" learned from the phone calls he had yet to make.

The scared consigner waited for a full 25 minutes until the agent called to say the National Archives were not interested in purchasing it. They stated again that the owner should donate the blood. The owner would not even consider donating, and claimed that as a fan of Reaganomics, he felt President Reagan would rather he sell than donate.

This Reaganomics fan lost out when the vial of blood was withdrawn from the auction in the midst of the action. In online auctions, the price rises over a set time period. But something very strange had happened: the owner had changed his mind about donating it to the National Archives. I do wonder if the FBI had anything to do with his sudden generosity.

At the time the owner was "motivated" to donate the blood, the last bid had climbed to more than $30,000. PFC called this donation to the Reagan Presidential Foundation "a considerable financial gesture from the consigner."

John Heubusch, Executive Director of the Foundation, said, "While we contend that the removal of the vial from the hospital laboratory and the U.S. auction sale...were not legal acts in our opinion, we are grateful to the current custodian of the vial for this generous donation to the Foundation, ensuring that President Reagan's blood remains out of public hands." A case in point: should you be unable to sell, you might always donate.

ANYONE FOR A SUBMERGED

# BUGATTI?

I HAVE A HUMDINGER OF A VINTAGE CAR
story, which will make any lover of old cars drool. It's a tale of a Type 22
Roadster at auction for $368,686 at Bonhams, Paris in January, 2010. How
did a Bugatti become submerged and remain underwater for so many
decades? This case study establishes *the value of persistence*.

This is a wild ride, akin to a crazy James Dean-Porsche 550 script. The
Roadster was sunk in 1936, in Lake Maggiore, Italy. The auction house
reported that the owner, a businessman, named Marco Schmuklerski, was
studying architecture at the famous École des Beaux-Arts when he bought
the car in 1925 in Paris. When in 1933 Schmuklerski decided to move to
Switzerland, he hadn't paid import duties on it, and research shows the car
was driven in Switzerland with French plates but never registered there.
Later, in 1936, when Schmuklerski left Switzerland, he placed the car with a
local contractor in Italy. And for those 11 years while it was on Swiss roads,

no one paid the duties, and the contractor refused to pay the overdue fees for his absent friend. Eventually, Swiss police tracked the car to Italy. At the time the Swiss often handled such non-registration malfeasance by destroying the car. So they rolled it into Lake Maggiore attached to a heavy chain, which was anchored to a secret place on land. If someone coughed up the duty tax it could then be hauled up and presented, dripping and muddy. But over so much time the water-logged car was forgotten and the chain corroded. The precious car fell to the very bottom of Lake Maggiore (more than 190 feet) and there it sat for 73 years.

In 1967, Ugo Pillon, an Italian diver, found the car in its watery parking spot, which was also his favorite diving place (though diving at 190 feet is almost unheard of). Since this was orderly Switzerland, the car had not been vandalized, unlike famous wrecks such as the *Titanic*. The front-enameled emblem with the wonderful Bugatti logo was gone, but 20% of the car was in perfect condition including all the fittings: wood, aluminum, brass, and rubber (possibly because of chilly waters).

In 2008, the local Italian sub-aqua (scuba) club sent out a young diver, Damiano Tamagni, to the soggy car, but, in a tragic event, a gang of young men killed him while he was on his way to the dive site.

So the members of the diving club, termed the Centro Sport Subacquei Salvataggio Ascona, met and determined that they would single-handedly raise the Bugatti in honor of the young man who had been murdered. And they proposed to auction the car when it surfaced, with the help of Bonhams Auction House in Paris, and to use the profits to set up a charity: Fondazione Damiano Tamagni. The foundation, named after the unfortunate young diver, was intended to fund the study of issues involving juvenile violence. The Roadster, so small and sporty and only as tall as the average man's hip, was still a huge feat to raise, though it was relatively light at 600 lbs.

The diver-mastermind behind this engineering feat was Jens Boerlin. A crane was employed and much intense rescue work followed, but when local law enforcement caught wind of the effort, the cops did the right thing. Instead of an arrest, the cops called the town dignitaries to throw a party when the Bugatti surfaced. Their local TV station heard about it, as did members of the Swiss Bugatti Club who used this event as an opportunity for a cavalcade road trip to Lake Maggiore. Great hampers of food, good

champagne, fine wines, and a band of musicians were loaded up to witness this Venus-car rising from the sea on July 12, 2009.

The great Ettore Bugatti worked for the Deutz Engine Company in Mannheim, Germany, until 1910 when he finished the Type 10, the first Bugatti, in his basement. Bugatti was in good company at Deutz, which was founded by Nikolaus Otto, the inventor of the 4-stroke internal combustion engine, back in 1848. It was Deutz that launched the legends such as Bugatti, Langen, Daimler, Maybach, L'Orange, and Benz. When he had finished the first Type 10, Bugatti loaded up his family and left for Alsace, France, to find a factory to build his cars. This particular first family car is now somewhere in California in the hands of a private owner.

The Type 13 Bugatti was the first real Bugatti, which began with the founding of Bugatti's marque (brand) in 1910. The first Type 13, built in Alsace, was entered in the Le Mans' French Grand Prix in 1911. It was the smallest car there, and termed *la baignoire* (bathtub). But after seven hours of racing, it took second place!

Only 435 cars of this type were produced, most with an eight-valve engine, but some with 16-valve heads. WWI interrupted production at Bugatti's Alsace factory and Ettore had to bury many cars and machines underground. When he later returned, he moved them to Milan to enter the Bugatti Brescia (the submerged Roadster is one such model) at Le Mans, beating every car.

But Bugatti was sadly disqualified that year simply because he had touched the car's radiator cap. Back he came in 1921 (without having touched the radiator cap), and the Brescia won all its races. This is the submerged Roadster's amazing pedigree.

In a great ending, when Bonham's auctioned the Bugatti for charity, the estimated value was $100,000 to $130,000. It sold for $368,686, despite missing parts and Bonham's advice that the chassis not be restored and that it should only be reproduced, in order for the wreck's preservation as sculpture. Bonham's catalogue admitted that the decision should be left to the lucky owner and we shall see.

## SURPRISES AT
# AUCTION

ACROSS THE POND, THE ENGLISH PAPER
*The Telegraph* reported the late Princess Diana's brother, Earl Spencer, held a gigantic sale of art and antiques at Spencer House, the family home. He was quoted as saying that he needed to sell because of the depressed English economy. Family heirlooms, including horse-drawn carriages and family souvenirs, were all carted out. But this was not just any estate sale. Earl Spencer remarkably offered a painting by Peter Paul Rubens and the painting was carried to London from the family's estate, Althorp (Diana's final resting place). The Rubens, *A Commander Being Armed for Battle* (17th century), sold for nine million pounds, or approximately $13.5 million. However, doubts have arisen that it is truly by Rubens, and leading art historians have questioned its provenance, declaring it "an uncomfortable Rubens." This case study underscores the *importance of consulting experts in any given field of material culture for provenance*, meaning who owned it and who sold

the object, over time. That provenance is pedigree.

While we're still in England, recently a British art dealer paid £120 (approximately $180) for what turned out to be an original 18th-century Gainsborough on eBay. Sir Thomas Gainsborough, the painter of the famous *Blue Boy* displayed at the Huntington, has been known to sell for three million dollars. Not bad for $180.

A playboy dressed in his best suit and driving a yellow Ferrari brought a stolen copy of a rare first edition of Shakespeare's plays into the world-famous Folger Shakespeare Library in Washington, DC. He'd hoped the library would buy the book, ostensibly to "pay for lifestyle problems." It was Raymond Scott, 53, the notorious international playboy (who lived with his mom). He was incredulous after the FBI seized him for dealing in valuable stolen merchandise. He reportedly kept asking the Folger librarians, "Would I be as stupid as to walk into the Shakespeare Library with a stolen first edition? I found this at a friend's house in Cuba!" You can imagine how he felt when the FBI ran his record and found that the nearly 400-year-old first folio had been suspected as stolen by Scott in 1988 from Durham University, England. Scott, who never

worked a day in his life and subsisted on a pension, claimed he was framed by Cuban Shakespeare experts.

As Scott was undergoing trial, the folio was placed on a pillow next to the jury. Experts discovered that pages had been ripped out and the entire folio damaged. It lost at least half its value of $4.5 million. Scott was then pronounced guilty and the judge gave him eight years at the Northumberland Prison for handling stolen goods. He died there in March of 2012. Previous to this, he'd been seen arriving at various court appearances in his own horse-drawn carriage led by a piper!

So do research the backstory of an object. I've often found that the stranger the backstory, the more probable the truth is lurking therein.

## OVER A

# BARREL

A CLIENT WROTE ME ABOUT HER 21 INCH high barrel with iron hoops. Inscribed on the barrel hoops is "Onix Prevents Athletes [sic] Foot." Having appraised for 30 years, I've seen many treasured antiques in my day but never have I come across a treasured athlete's foot medicine container. Still, J. treasures it, so here goes a valuation of the Onix Athlete's Foot Barrel. This case study emphasizes the *wide range of collectibles, wherein each object has a unique history, often accompanied by a dedicated collector base*. If you decide to collect in a specific area of material culture, try to become the *expert*.

Barrels themselves have been used as containers for bulk goods such as wine, beer, spirits, and nails for over 2,000 years and are still made by coopers. Barrels have lost their position as the number one transport vessel, but considering their longevity, they've only recently lost their place in history. At the beginning of the 20th century, containers changed all that. The corrugated fiberboard/cardboard box was invented and then the barrel lost

further ground with the invention of pallets.

What are barrels made of? Wood is best: through heating, the wood is secured with metal bands or staves. This technique originated in ancient Phoenicia with boat builders, who heated and bent wood. The first time the barrel made literary history was in the 1st century when Pliny the Elder wrote about Alpen winemakers (Gauls) who shipped wine to Rome in specially designed wooden containers. It's the distinct convex shape with a bulge in the middle which makes the barrel unique. It's easy to roll on its side (less friction), easy to change direction, and the shape distributes stress evenly. J.'s barrel has four hoops made of galvanized iron but they're not equally distributed. Most notably, the second from the bottom is nearest the full swell of the barrel. Coopers call this the head or chime hoop. Before the development of galvanized iron, barrel coopers used flexible wood bits called withies, and in those days coopers needed more than four wooden hoops. If wood encircled the barrel, the full top and bottom third of each barrel had to be secured with withies.

Before this chapter places your appraiser over a barrel, I'll stipulate a value for J.'s Athlete's Foot Barrel. I was unable to find an Onix company or Onix medication, but a similar late 19th-century wooden barrel advertising Hires Root Beer sold for $300. I put J.'s prize barrel at $500, for oddities' sake. If you can't find a direct comparable sale, try to look for a similar object which has *been sold*—not a "would you take it for" offered price.

En in Silk by Thomas Stevens, Inventor and Manufacturer, Coventry and London, (Reg

The Lady Godiva Procession.

## THE AMAZING STEVENGRAPH AND THE JACQUARD

# LOOM

MY CLIENT N.H. SENT A TEXTILE WEAVING
with a story dating from the Middle Ages and from a town called Rüti in
what is now Switzerland. Engineers discovered that the adjacent Jona River
was perfect for hydropower, which they harnessed to water mills for textile
manufacturing. This case study shows *how researching an object often leads to
a history, economics, sociological, and anthropological expedition.* Your job is to
dig out an object's unique story, which you may assume will become more
interesting (and therefore more valuable) over time.

The theme of N.H.'s late 19th-century textile is medieval Swiss and
depicts William Tell with his young son. The Tell legend dates back to 1475,
when a country scribe referenced Tell as a freedom fighter in 1291 against
the Hapsburgs (Austria's ruling family) and their impending domination of
the Swiss. Tell's legend persisted throughout the turbulent 19th century into
WWII as a symbol of rebellion against tyranny. We all remember the legend:
a nasty Hapsburg governor planted his hat on a pole in a Swiss town square

and ordered the townspeople to bow before it. Tell and his son would not bow so the governor ordered the execution of both, to be withheld only if Tell could shoot an apple off his son's head with his crossbow. Tell succeeded and then promptly killed the governor with an arrow. Tell's challenge to authority has since reverberated throughout every era. Writers such as the Brothers Grimm (1816), Antoine-Marin Lemierre (1766: think of the American and French revolutions), Goethe (1795), Rossini (*William Tell* opera, 1829), and Friedrich von Schiller (1804) all wrote about Tell, and a play about him has been performed every year since 1947 at Interlaken, Switzerland.

N.H.'s textile is part of that legend's fame. The weaving was done on a silk Jacquard loom, a mechanical device controlling countless loops and pulleys to weave patterns into textiles. In fact, N.H.'s piece was done on one of the world's first "computers"! Each entry of these threads was controlled by a punch card perforated for every single woven line of the picture, much like analog computer punch cards. An image as small as a bookmark woven with a Jacquard loom still required 6,000 perforated cards.

In England, where this technique developed, the weaving style is a "Stevengraph" after its inventor Thomas Stevens of Canterbury, England (Canterbury also became a center of textile manufacturing). The term is now used in general for silk pictures like N.H.'s.

What is the value of N.H.'s 19th-century Stevengraph? A 20th-century copy by the same Rüti factory sold for $60. The palette is called *en griselle:* a picture executed in monochrome in shades of white to gray to black. This technique is most often used in imitation of classical sculpture and pen and ink drawings, or executed in copperplate etchings as portrait heads (and, of course, on Stevengraphs).

Today they're not popular in the antique market but they represent the technology leading up to the modern computer (the old analog punch cards). I suspect value will grow, so N.H. should hang on to this silk weaving. Thus, we learn an object can cross into stories about *process* as opposed to presence. This one may be worth more as just an example of early analog computing than as a work of art.

## PORCELAIN AS MORE THAN MEETS THE
# EYE

Biscuit porcelain is unglazed white ceramic ware, and is seen most often in the huge output of 19th-century bisque doll heads. Biscuit is the name for pottery which has been fired but not glazed. Biscuit is fired at a lower temperature than bone china porcelain, and biscuit earthenware absorbs water and watercolor, so figures were easily painted or glazed. They were also less expensive to manufacture and cheaper to purchase than porcelain. But the fact that they were decorated with saccharine colors is the problem today. By today's standards, the colors are cloyingly sugar-coated. These candy-box pastel figures don't sell for what similar, but uncolored, porcelains might bring. Still, I predict tastes will change and their sweet colors will make a comeback. This case study highlights *objects which were once highly-prized and collected, but have fallen into market disfavor.* Your job is to guess if the market will ever fall in love with them again.

The history of biscuit porcelain began in 18th-century France, culminating in the major French expositions, those huge trade fairs boasting thousands

of French inventions and designs throughout the 19th century. One of the best known biscuit makers was Gilles Jeune of Vion+Baury. He was known for making a splash at two major expositions, and in 1844 he triumphed with what were called "mantle garniture."

Mantle garniture were typically fancy ornate figures, clocks, or candelabra, primarily in use as mantlepiece displays. By the mid-19th century, mantle garniture might hold a clock and a couple *objets d'art:* vases (candlesticks, and urns) all promoting a virtuous message. A young, half-nude goddess as a candlestick figure pouring water to accompany a classical clock might have suggested "time and beauty flow." A clock featuring a chariot recalled Icarus's prideful fall from the heavens. This inherent moralism was part and parcel of 19th-century decorative arts and biscuit art (*bisque*) followed suit.

The second triumph of Gilles Jeune was at a large 1858 exposition in Toulouse, France, where he displayed busts of the Emperor Napoléon III and his empress. He also created elevated figural groups such as the *Mother of Lovers, The Dressing of Venus,* and *Rachael.* These subjects suggested moral lessons, as well as providing an avenue for nudity—not generally much on view in 1858.

My client L.L.'s figure, probably fashioned by Vion+Baury, is seated on a swing and displays the titillating combination of the era's moralism and voyeurism. Take the mother of all swing-themed *objets d'art:* Fragonard's *The Swing* or *Happy Accidents of the Swing.* In this suggestive painting of the 18th century, the young man lounges beneath his young lady, watching her swing (and perhaps waiting for the wind to blow her skirts up).

Naturally, one has to pump one's legs to cause the swing to move, so there are all kinds of lurid suggestions here. All this could be imagined whenever a Victorian person saw a shapely female figure of beauty on a swing.

Swinging female figures were often placed with ropes on a light fixture or atop windowsills. Their purpose was to add decoration, as well as to prompt the imagination. If designed by Gilles Jeune (which, by its fine expertise, I think it was) L.L.'s swing girl is worth $800, but only to a Bisque collector who has hedged their bets that Bisque will make a return.

## NOTHING MORE HIDEOUS THAN THIS

# CHAIR

I RECEIVED A PHOTO OF AN OLD CHAIR from client C.P featuring an ornate, mahogany affair with a carved and cartouche-crested top rail. It features a pierced and carved back splat with throne arms, ending in seated-lion caryatids. All is supported on lion-faced cabriole legs culminating in hairy paws. This is a Rococo Revival chair and this is the language I was taught at Christie's Auction House in Manhattan to describe antique furniture (and used in auction catalogues). You may not recognize the chair from that description, so I'll describe it as overblown, heavy, and hideous. And worth about $200. This case study focuses on *furniture which, although well-constructed and painstakingly carved, is out of favor in today's marketplace*. It's a lesson in the fickleness and volatility of the antique market, since tastes can change on a dime. It also illustrates the influence of architecture on furniture design. This chair reflects the era perfectly.

Rococo Revival was the most popular style of furniture and architecture for 50 years beginning in the 1850s. It's the contribution of Napoléon III, first president of France's Second Republic, who crowned himself Emperor of France's Second Empire. The First Empire belonged solely to his uncle Napoléon I. Napoléon III of the House of Bonaparte was a reformer. Interestingly, the current head of the House of Bonaparte, Jean-Christophe (Prince Napoléon), is a 28-year-old investment banker at New York's Morgan Stanley firm.

His ancestor Napoléon III redesigned Paris with the assistance of engineer Georges-Eugène Haussmann. The noted Avenue de l'Opéra leads directly to the Opera House. Beginning in Paris in the year 1854, Haussmann and Napoléon III cut through centuries of old buildings to create 50 miles of new avenues, all connecting to central parts of Paris.

They were in Rococo Revival style, known in France as the Second Empire. Napoléon III's style was a more grandly imagined classic French Empire style than that of his Uncle Napoléon I, and all the world tried to follow suit.

The spikily mustached Napoléon III and his Empress Eugénie led a glittering social life hosting lavish parties amid opulent surroundings. The world assumed if it was French,

it must be the last word in fashion. Thus, C.P.'s chair is a luxurious, aristocratic specimen and today highly unpopular. It's meant to tell us about the sitter's classy rear end!

Rococo Revival spread from France to Germany, then to England, and sifted down to the U.S. mansions of East Coast robber barons, who were enamored of anything hinting at French culture.

The style trickled down to the American middle class, and was especially valued by those who had come from nothing and made a little money running dirty coal-fired factories. They craved luxurious trappings to declare their aristocratic tastes, though they were bereft of all class or title. They simply hoped ornate, fancy furniture would elevate their status.

C.P.'s chair dates from the 1860s and is likely part of a dining suite with many equally overdone, obnoxious dining chairs as well as a huge, ponderous dining table. The concept all but screams, "Show grand, and you are grand."

Note: Upon the birth of my son, my secretary instructed me to ditch the French-style furniture in his bedroom, for fear it would make him an effeminate monster. I'm happy to say this furniture's only effect was to turn him into a Zen minimalist. He hates antiques.

## A MEDIEVAL CARVED WOOD

# ICON

A GREAT SANTA BARBARA MONEY GURU
and client called J.P. held a financial planning seminar that I attended. J.P.
kindly mentioned that attendees could contact me to establish value on their
estates for planning purposes. One attendee sent photos from her grandmother's estate and a particular image caught my eye for its age, integrity,
and beauty. It was a German-carved (oak or limewood) polychrome figure of
Saint Catherine. If we count the number of artistic saint representations, she
is possibly the second most important female saint after Saint Barbara. This
case study illustrates how *certain objects' worth is enhanced by their particular
geographic region*. Do your research and market accordingly.

The cult of Saint Catherine likely originated in the 15th or 16th century and
I believe J.P.'s object dates to the 16th century. I saw traces of gilding on top of a
red glaze—highly typical of the late-medieval German style. It's the Northern
Renaissance style as opposed to the Italian Renaissance style (geographically
the Southern Renaissance).

Above: Tilman Riemenschneider, *Grieving Women,* detail

The gilding has a distinct pattern to it and I don't believe the little saint was meant to be polychromed (painted or enameled in more than one color).

Monochromatic works of saint carvings are far more common and were often mounted as altarpieces. How do I know this little figure was most likely incorporated into a baroque altarpiece? Because her proportions are very elongated—a deliberate technique for adoration from slightly below. The swaying folds of her drapery also indicate she was part of a larger setting which may have been set in an architectural niche.

Her clothing closely follows the S-curve of her body, as she shifts weight to one leg. Another clue to a niche-mounted sculpture is that she's not well-finished on the back side. The cringing pose was often reserved for saints whose martyrdom resembles Saint Barbara's.

Saint Catherine was a beautiful,

long-haired maiden, the daughter of the 4th-century King and Queen of Egypt. J.P.'s figure has the same long hair and feminine curves. Catherine had refused to marry a non-Christian, insisting she'd remain a virgin and marry only Christ. The pagan Emperor Maxentius had proposed marriage and planned to break her on that infamous wheel.

When faced with a wheel of torture, Catherine prayed and the wheel disappeared. The Emperor Maxentius, confused and infuriated, had her beheaded. Saint Catherine was said to have remained beautiful even after death. Apocrypha has it that Saint Catherine's body was discovered in the year 800 AD at the base of Mt. Sinai, and that her hair had continued to grow. The cult of Saint Catherine was born.

What is the worth of J.P.'s lovely saint figure? The most famous of all Northern Renaissance German wood icon-makers was Tilman Riemenschneider (1460–1531) and the last saint figure carved by him was sold in 2008 at Sotheby's of New York for $6,313,000. So I asked J.P. to bring that little sculpture into my office, so I could see it in person. It turned out to be a 19th-century copy of a 16th-century sculpture. The carving was too crisp to be really old

and this is why it's so important to hold the actual piece. J.P. sold it in Santa Barbara, a city named for the patron saint, for $1,000. But what if it was a great copy?

It all depends upon the *type* of copy. Is it in the *style* of a certain artist or is it from their circle—which means over years and years within the artist's lifetime. There are two types of "copies," which are not really copies at all: Tilman Riemenschneider founded a school of Northern Renaissance sculptural naturalism and those students carved in the same style.

They are called his "circle": a few generations of students either taught by the master, or taught by those same students. All qualify as the "circle" of a master.

A sculpture from the circle of Riemenschneider is now worth at least $4,000 to $6,000. But a 19th-century sculpture following the style of Riemenschneider's circle or of the master himself, is considered more distant from the artist's hand—an important criteria of "closeness" and essential to value. Thus this little, crisp sculpture is classified as "in the style of the master" and worth far less at only $500 to $800. J.P certainly targeted a great geographic area for his sale!

## HOW TO BUY, SELL, INSURE, AND

# AUCTION

In THIS PART, I TALK TURKEY IN A DOWN
market to discuss the hard facts of how the art market works in those times
when you must sell your treasures. Many people go through stressful financial
times, and although we may not like to think about it, it's sometimes necessary to take a sober look at our material assets.

I've been struck by certain changes in my appraisal business: my wealthiest
clients back in 2009 asked for a complete assessment of their art and antiques
in case the bottom were to fall out. When our wealthiest neighbors were worried, they immediately ordered an appraisal to know what to sell. This case
study includes a *short guide on just that: how and what to sell.*

Periodic reality checks may have you contemplating streamlining your life by
divesting yourself of certain things and getting down to what really matters. I
myself have had occasion to simplify my circumstances and hope the following,
gathered from clients' questions in a down market, will provide encouragement.

First, look at your art and antiques with the knowledge that whatever you paid may be irrelevant as a seller. And the only exception is the very top end of the art and antique market, which I predict will flourish because those collectors and buyers are driven to buy the very best—even if it means selling both grandmothers to raise the capital!

Value is established at an auction house by examining the price of a work in recent sales. At the big auction houses, where their appraisers suggest a margin in which to sell a work—called an "auction estimate range"—their auctioneers may reduce the top-end figure of that auction if they feel the market for that artist is floundering.

When a market is truly poor (as in the first quarter of 2009, when there were only 79 sales worldwide in which someone paid over a million dollars for a work of art) the estimates are much tighter and much more conservative. In 2009, artwork fell to the middle or bottom end. Thus, the middle and bottom ends showed greater activity, but here also the estimates of value were much lower than previous to 2008. Therefore, the number of paintings with an estimate of $5,000 or less in 2009 was 10% higher than in 2008. The middle of the art market,

which is considered to be works at or above $50,000, was weak in 2009 but the bottom (those works which are valued at under $2,000) was actually quite active and strong. All this upheaval led to a change in auction house policies, of course.

As of 2009, all the auction houses ceased guaranteeing a price that had to be realized or the work would be pulled from the auction. Previously, the work reverted back to the owner if that guaranteed price was not met, but today, once you enter a painting in an auction, whatever price it brings is what you get. That guaranteed price used to be termed the "reserve."

Add to this the fact that buyers are extra cautious and auction houses are closing. The very rich of China, Russia, India, and Turkey, who are fast becoming big, new players in the market, are wealthy but they're art cautious. In fact, after the first quarter of 2009, the world had 300 fewer billionaires. The spring of 2008, conversely, which saw multi-million dollar sales, reflected seven previous consecutive years of growth. In one year (2009) we went from peak to trough. The genre of art that was most affected was work by living artists born after 1945, that is, contemporary artists. Regional paintings such as those by early 20th-century

California plein air artists held up in regions they represent. Thus, we learn from experiencing one of the worst art markets in history to do thorough research first.

One must understand the *whole* of the market and compare it with the type of market for your specific object. If you are considering liquidating, understand that you'll need to research the value of your pieces in the secondary market (auction), from whence the term "liquidation" actually derives. Here's a really useful research site: Prices4Antiques.com, wherein objects' fair market value can be found. A layperson can peruse objects in photos prior to reading descriptions. One needn't know everything about its history, but the first step is to understand the look of the object, its "style," in order to research value.

Many clients say "I saw an object like mine on *Antiques Roadshow* and it went for $500,000." But that is not the value for selling the item: it may only be the value for insuring it. And those values are *very* different—especially today. That single $500,000 item may be the best of its kind, but an item which appears as the best might only be a good reproduction and worth almost nothing. So beware of judging by outward appearance.

After you know your object's style, research its date, provenance, and historical background.

Second, since you may not really know what you own, compile an inventory of the items. List those you feel will steadily increase in value and save them for your heirs or a time when you really need to sell. If an item has become popular in the art and antique market and continues to rise in value, hold on to it. You'll see this trend on sites such as Prices4Antiques.com wherein you can find the dates of each sale. Track the rise and fall in prices paid over time, and hold onto items which you believe will increase. You may be surprised by some: neither modern Native American material nor contemporary hand-drawn maps are produced in the same way as they were ages past. What is no longer an art form, using the same techniques and materials, but created by the same culture (such as these two genres), is not always of value now.

Third, notice what is selling and where. Then try somewhere else. I would not suggest eBay for specialized sale items such as regional paintings. For collectibles which are selling nationwide, eBay works well (old toys, well-known print artists, and pop collectibles). But neither eBay

nor Craigslist is good for everything. When you have something special, research collectors' clubs online and even email them. There are clubs for just about anything: the Hummel Club, the Cut Glass Club, and even the Zippo Lighter Club. The more targeted your sales pitch, the higher the price.

Fourth, selling locally to galleries, antique shops, fellow collectors, and friends is a good idea and helpful to local shops. The number one issue with selling online is how you actually receive payment, so selling locally can be a more trustworthy avenue. But that doesn't mean you should trust a dealer's quote and nor should you always accept the first price a dealer proposes.

You need to research and perhaps consult an independent third party. Clients may not realize that dealers and auctions specialize. I.M. Chait Auctions in California mainly handles Asian art and archaeological material, while Eldred's Auction in Maine focuses on nautical items. These houses insure a great audience for specialized items and some will even pay for shipping an item of any size, if it's not local.

Lastly, what if you have a higher, middle-market, Victorian antique piece which is much too large and unwieldy to move? Often I run into this when clients ask about selling and my advice is to give it away.

If you're in a financial situation in which you can benefit from a charitable, non-cash contribution as a deduction against taxes (if nothing else), then claim the item's fair-market value. Get good tax advice since rules for charitable giving keep tightening. The IRS will be monitoring haphazard deduction claims but it may work out to your advantage to donate.

Remember to document and take photos of all items you consider valuable and send them to those close to you. Ask what they may want before you sell. I'm continually amazed by the items my clients' children consider valuable and, on the other hand, what they absolutely do not want! It often has nothing to do with monetary value. A photo inventory is always necessary for insurance. I have my own personal inventory of what I own, along with pictures of myself holding the items my son would like.

It's sentimental, but there is such a thing. We need to retain a loving attitude, do good research, and keep a cool head. One can get through anything. Even downsizing!

## LESSONS TO LEARN IN A STRONG

# MARKET

SINCE YOU READ ABOUT MY ADVICE FOR
a downmarket, this is a case study on *buying in an upmarket*. The hardcore
collectors who'd sell their grandmothers for a work by their favorite artist
came back in 2010 and big auction house sales reflected it. At the end of
the prestigious *Impressionist and Modern Art Sale*, Christie's and Sotheby's
posted a combined revenue up 205% ($457.7 million sold on May 4–5, 2010)
compared to the total sales in 2000. By the end of the *Contemporary Art Sale*,
revenue was up 230% ($368.5 million on May 11–12, 2010) over the sales
figures of 2009. In fact, 12 new artists' sales records were set, including $95
million paid for Picasso's lascivious *Dora Maar*.

The art market, as I've learned, is both a classic economic indicator as
well as a hub for addicts who need another fix when the buying is good. So
when those addicts see the market surging back, they lose no time and buy

again. Or, they enter into the good market to sell *off* the bottom pieces in their collection. This applies more to the top end of the market (where the real addicts are) than the middle. In 2010 (hallelujah!) the high-end international art market showed real confidence in buying for investment purposes.

In May, 2010, a 1980 *Self-Portrait* by Andy Warhol owned by the American designer Tom Ford sold at Sotheby's for $29 million. A Mark Rothko red painting sold for $28 million—all record-breakers! A good percentage of contemporary works actually sold for amounts over what auction house estimates had predicted: *Untitled (Stardust)* by Jean-Michel Basquiat was estimated to sell at $800,000 to $2,500,000 and ended up selling for $6,400,000.

As I predicted, when the market returned and art sold again, the savvy collectors began to sell. For example, the estate of Michael Crichton, author of *Jurassic Park*, sold Jasper Johns's *(American) Flag*, an early 1960s piece never before seen at auction, for $25.5 million. These astonishing high-end market results usually point to effervescence in art sales for the not-so-wealthy collector as well. However, the old adage is still true: it's just as much work to sell a $50 piece as it is to sell a $500 piece. In a true upmarket, some smaller auction houses and galleries which consign will raise the consignment fee and set limits on what they'll handle. That consignment fee is called a per-piece minimum. The big auction house minimum has gone up around $5,000 per item, and some smaller houses won't even accept things which they've pre-valued for less than $2,000. But many of my clients want to buy and need to sell items that should be priced less than $300. What is the fate of low-end material in an up or "resurfacing" market?

I've noticed some clear trends. The small-amount seller is really hard-pressed to find an outlet. Where I live, pickers (professional estate and garage sale buyers) visit local estate sales with about $1,000 cash, only to find that they didn't bring enough moolah. Big-ticket items like great paintings and antique silver sets are now being offered at these sales because auction houses have set limits. Previously, those quality items which were under $5,000 could have gone to auction, but no longer. When a seller must downsize, I often appraise valuable donations which have no place to go but thrift stores.

I also see far more "free" placards

on curbside furniture. The current trend is to sell and shop online, but not everyone has the patience or time for the necessary photos, verbiage, shipping, and tracking. Some of the collectors who wish to downsize have no choice but to become dealers, so they set up at local swap meets. Few folks have the stamina or desire to get up at four AM to haul their wares to a three-day flea market.

In 2010, at the high end of the art and antique markets (top 15% of sales), we saw a giant boom. This trend continues through today. When the market is up, everyone wants to sell. But the middle-to-low end will stagnate. What many cities need are more local outlets for those used items valued at $50 to $5,000, because in this price range, the general feeling is that it costs more to sell an item than what it's worth. The dearth of good places to sell inexpensive objects continues in 2016: there are few outlets, for example, on California's Central Coast for middle-of-the-road art and antique sales. Thus, estate sale professionals make a killing, as do people who have enough storage for more collectibles in their homes (or are just addicts). In such a resurgent art market, the pickins will be great.

# WHAT TO
# BEQUEATH

Ｄ**URING A TIME WHEN I HAD NOWHERE**
to live other than in a hotel, my mother in Chicago very kindly asked me and
my East Coast business partner to stay with her until I heard news about
my house, which had suffered damage in Santa Barbara's 2009 Jesusita fire.
So we two professional appraisers descended upon my 80-year-old mother,
Elinor, in her assisted living community. As I was getting ready for bed
(there is something comforting about getting ready for bed in your mother's
house), my Mom asked me "What do you want from this place after I am
gone?" This case study deals with *everyone with older parents who are hinting
they want to give things away*. Mom's question gripped me with fear and
forced me to think as an appraiser about her material goods.

First is the parent personality type who just wants you to have items that
have been in the family a long time, or something sentimental to remind you

of it. Second is the parent who wants you to have something valuable, as long as all the siblings have an item of equal value. Third is the type who worries endlessly about how to divide up art, antiques, and jewelry (and goes crazy thinking about it).

One client of mine had divided a fine collection of antique gold charms from a sweet antique bracelet and then distributed the charms among six siblings so that all inherited equally. This ruined the gift as the charms no longer belonged to the bracelet.

Some clients' parents separated paired paintings, divided five-piece silver tea sets, or portioned out matching sets of china. As a parent, you have a delicate task: choosing between being fair and maintaining the collection's integrity. Attempting to be equitable can be frustrating and emotionally fraught so I urge those with older parents to take the lead when possible. Here are some instructive guides with actual background cases.

I'll begin with varying types of siblings: the first is the type who only desires sentimental items (family pictures, cards, letters, etc.). Second is the one who wants the good stuff—good being code for valuable. Of course, there's nothing wrong with that, and sometimes value in the marketplace is also family value. Third is the sibling who won't face the fact that aged parents pass away and refuse to have a conversation about "stuff" with parents. I've learned this emotional, avoidant sibling may be the stinker after the fact!

Now let's look at three situations in heirship. A parent might die intestate, without a trust or will (which makes the government all the wealthier). Secondly, a trust is created for the assets, but it usually excludes art and antiques unless the client and attorney insist a work of art *must* be in the estate. In either case, a parent may bequeath objects without necessarily assessing their value. But savvy sibling(s) will encourage parents to *talk* about their items and one solution is to order a professional appraisal to ascertain value (not always, as you'll see from my mother's case). The overriding concern is *how* to give things away, and value is often of prime concern.

So what to do? For elderly parents, I will respond to this quandary at two levels, both of which have worked for my family. (Disclaimer: in all cases of heirship issues, check with your attorney!)

The first scenario involves my mother's objects which are only of

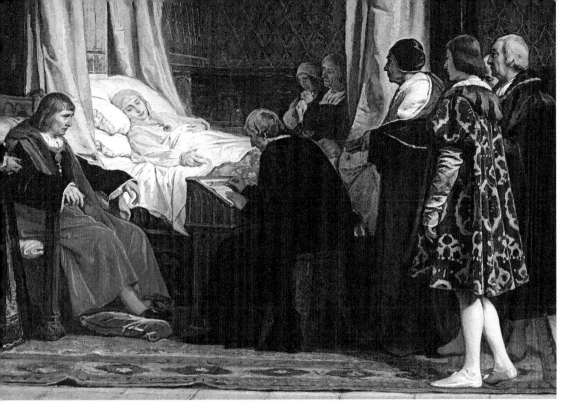

average household value, with some sentimental objects included. Mom has a trust which does not necessarily include personal possessions of her art and porcelain collectibles.

She might label what she wants to give each of her children with something as simple as their name on masking tape affixed to an object. She has determined value by asking what these objects would bring if they were to be sold at auction. If my mother were concerned about gifts of equal value, after speaking with her attorney she might ask me to draw up an appraisal. She could then designate according to *equitable* value.

This is literally called an "appraisal for equitable distribution," and requires the estimation of fair market value, which is defined as the most common price paid in the most appropriate market. Therefore, for my mother's objects, the fair market value would be the price paid by those attending local estate sales.

Once who gets what is decided, she's left with what she perceives as quite a lot of *stuff*—which worries her. She's reluctant to leave a household full of objects which she has determined we won't want.

This is also a cautionary tale: as I've expressed my appreciation for certain objects in her house, it has surprised her. It is important to give voice to your favorite objects. It's a window onto a life and you may be surprised at the stories behind a little porcelain frog or ballerina.

At this stage in her life, my mother does not have the same energy she once did, and feels compelled to downsize. Many of my older clients worry about leaving too much behind after they die, especially those who have had to handle their own parents' estates, or have served as a best friend's executor. To be an executor is one of life's most difficult assignments, and parents worry about saddling those close to them.

After my mother consults with her attorney, for peace of mind, I asked that she label her pieces with our names, and draw up a letter to her attorney and/or executor about who gets what, with no dollar figures mentioned. That assignment of visible objects alleviates concern about any crushing estate work left later.

The second level involves parents who own valuable collections. My advice is for adult children to prepare an estate for appraisal by following the *Four Piles Rule* (my "trademark!").

First, help parents separate objects into four categories by using different color stickers to identify them. Pile One is items to be donated, Pile Two is objects to be kept in the household, Pile Three is what will be bequeathed, and Pile Four is what may be donated as a legacy to non-profits (museum, church, university). An appraiser may then assess the value in Piles Three and Four.

When the dollar figures are set down on paper, the decision as to who gets what becomes very clear. Sometimes clients ask me to project a value into the future; for example, using an artist's sales records for the past 40 years to project future sales. This also aids in the decision process, especially if a museum bequest is at issue.

Usually those who collect will have an idea of their objects' values, but a professional appraisal might bring them up to speed on current

*For objects not designated for any of the children, each planned visit to a parent might include four hours dedicated to culling through a single category of object. More than valuation, this is saying goodbye.*

market trends. Older parents can decide if they want to go forward with an appraisal written only for the heirs and set that up in an equitable distribution format. I have seen many creative attorneys prepare such equitable distribution documents in expert ways, and one of the most interesting parts of my job is presenting an appraisal for such distribution with both attorney and family present.

The key to "What to Bequeath" is advance planning. Ask for the assistance of your parents' accountant and attorney sooner rather than later. Then hire a professional organizer and professional appraiser.

Human nature being what it is, planning usually starts with the *least* valuable of what's in the house. But the dross needs to be cleared so that parents can focus on objects of *real* value. Start this process and use my personal experience to sound out your parents. I've sat in on *many* sibling meetings and know they can easily go south when money is involved (and old rivalries are ignited). Families in grief do not deserve that.

Here are two interesting stories about two very different families who failed to follow this advice. The first one involves a wealthy mother who passed away leaving three daughters. She'd drawn up a will and trust, yet either she didn't know of or didn't tell her attorney of a very valuable painting. The attorney of one daughter invited me to the house to write up an appraisal in settling the estate. This clever daughter seized the painting, telling us: "Dr. Stewart doesn't need to include this in the estate appraisal; Mom gave it to me a few Christmases past."

Another attorney in attendance asked for this daughter to produce the Christmas card which ostensibly gifted her the painting. When the daughter looked crestfallen, he said, "She didn't give you a Christmas card giving you this gift after she died, did she?" If I divulged the painting's artist you might admire the daughter's chutzpah, however.

In the second case, a family of two brothers and two sisters in radically different economic circumstances discovered the magnitude of their parents' Asian porcelain collection. The executor had no idea that the collection might be valuable until I showed up.

Asian porcelain can be both classic and valuable: a 15th-century Ming vase can be reproduced in all its beauty fairly accurately today, and it takes a real pro to establish value in Chinese art. It was evident to me that just *one* pair of objects in the estate had a value of over $5,000: a pair of joss sticks (porcelain incense holders used on an altar) in the shape of elephants. Then a strange thing happened. These four siblings envisioned the entire household as rare and valuable and so requested that I appraise everything. Down to their mother's favorite eggcup! That eggcup was worth a few dollars, but what ensued was a battle royale between two sisters and it continues to this day.

These four siblings began my interview claiming to be incredibly close and easygoing about the estate's distribution. But as soon as they scented the possibility of lucre, they began to tangle.

So I strongly urge holding a "stuff" conversation with your parents and rehearsing the conversation with a friend or bringing a like-minded sibling. Do it for your parents' sake. If thirty years of my older clients' concerns are any indicator, they *do* worry about this!

## A COLLECTING
# STRATEGY

I HAVE BEEN POKING AROUND ESTATE
sales, antique shows, garage sales, and thrift stores for way too many years
now. As a matter of fact, my first job was as an assistant to a farm auction in
my native Illinois when I was 13. So this case study offers a few *hints gathered
in my 30 years of picking and assessing value.* The first hint comes from my old
appraisal professor in New York who mentored me for eight years while I
was in training. When I became a certified appraiser, he left me with these
parting words as a gift, "Elizabeth, always remember: old things look old."
Now this may not sound brilliant, but it is. Old things do show the wear of
human hands. Old things, if they have a bottom side, will show wear even
if they're wood, glass or bronze. Old things fade over time (for example,

the back of an old canvas) and they won't display the same fading pattern overall. The best way to tell if a piece of furniture is old is to look inside a drawer and then compare the outside of the drawer with the inside to see if the wood is lighter. The inside should be darker because it wasn't exposed to the air or light as much as the outside. Look again to see if new hardware holes were cut for new pulls. If so, the piece has been around awhile. These are the type of signs which indicate whether a piece of furniture is old.

Old things feel worn in the hand. I swear (and give me leave to make this point) old things do talk back when they're held. Sometimes I actually have to ask them, "What are you?" And they usually answer because old things have a different energy. Take a pair of eyeglasses which belonged to someone who is now gone. Hold them and you will get a buzz. Or try holding a coin that has long been out of circulation. Soon you'll feel its own old energy.

Second hint: if you should go to thrift store to pick up something you can later resell, you'll become an expert in one or two areas of collecting. For example: not many know about Australian Aboriginal art called Dream Painting. As this is a fading art form, it's getting rarer. I once picked up such a canvas for $10. After researching the artist, I then emailed a gallery in Australia specializing in this type of art and discovered such a piece sells there for $11,000. I am not going to sell it, because I love it, but it's nice to make such a score.

My New York mentors at the Appraiser's Association of America, of which I'm a certified member, would advise me to concentrate on one area (*any* one) and research just that field for a few years. This is excellent training and they insisted I follow it. So my mentor designated an area about which I knew nothing, and he knew enough about me to realize that I wouldn't be interested in collecting marbles. Yet for two years I hunted for glass marbles, as asked.

The assignment worked well as I focused so narrowly in one area that I became a bit of an expert in others: turn-of-the-century children's hobbies, glass-blowing techniques, the particular composition of various styles of glass, the economics of various turn-of-the-century glass factories and their cities, the patterns of wear to be expected on glass materials, the way certain colors are produced in glass, the diseases common to glass blowers at the time, etc. When my two-year assignment had finally passed, I was thrilled to no longer search for marbles again!

Above: Dale Chihuly, Glass Art, Kew Gardens, London *(Pache99z)*

But because I'd taught myself how to look and research only a specific area of material culture, I used that skill and transferred it to a wide range of collecting. I suggest becoming a connoisseur of a single area when you start learning the collecting ropes. Narrow your field instead of collecting a variety.

This same theory works for value. The narrower the field in which you sell, the higher the price you receive. For example, a gent has every *Playboy Magazine* from 1960 to 1980, but is missing September 1974. He has looked everywhere and can't find a copy. What do you think he'd pay for that copy? Much more than a casual

voyeur at a yard sale, who has little interest in collecting the series.

Here's another hint: when hunting, go with your gut. When you enter an estate sale or a thrift shop, go to the first section to which you're pulled, even if it's not one of your favorite haunts. There's good reason your gut is telling you to go there. When I had spent all my money on a plane ticket to attend my stepbrother's wedding in an exotic place, I had none left for a formal gown (and this was definitely black-tie). So I went to my Goodwill and followed my gut to the back of the store's big mirror where things are tried on. I rifled through a huge pile lying on the floor at the foot

> *But because I'd taught myself how to look and research only a specific area of material culture, I used that skill and transferred it to a wide range of collecting. I suggest becoming a connoisseur of a single area when you start learning the collecting ropes. Narrow your field instead of collecting a variety.*

of the mirror and, lo and behold, I found a coiled-up, handmade, 1920s Fortuny silk gown. This stunner of a dress is pink with five-panel pleated "Delphos," created by Mariano Fortuny y Madrazo (Italian/Spanish, 1871–1949), and is worth $2,000. Amazingly, it fit me perfectly. I go with my instincts.

Finally, remember that whatever goes around, will come around. I appraised a client's great artwork collection and called her to come by to pick up her appraisal, as I'd wanted to show her a painting in my office. Incredibly, this client also collects Aboriginal art.

That was a Monday morning and it had only been the Saturday before when I'd visited a thrift store and followed my instincts. I'd duly tromped over piles of mismatched dishes to finally pull out a little platter. It was actually a painting on ceramic in the shape of a fish, and was marked at $3.99. It spoke to me and I thought, no, don't be silly, Elizabeth, and I put it down. But as soon as I did, I saw another woman eyeing that shelf and the same platter, so I rushed over and grabbed it back. My client came to the office the following Monday and, as she sat down, pointed to the platter and asked, "When did you buy that dish?" Notice she did not ask where, because she already knew where it had come from. She'd just donated that dish and a big box of other Australian pieces to Goodwill the previous week. She and her husband were connoisseurs of Australian art but simply had too much inventory and wanted to weed their collection.

This is becoming a connoisseur. Decrease the bottom end of the collection and build up the top.

(Durova)

## A NATURAL DISASTERS

# LESSON

THIS IS A LESSON FOR ALL THE FUTURE: record what you consider valuable in your household setting. This case study *encourages using both a still camera and video to record* these: the item, the price paid, the provenance (story of where and from whom an item was acquired), along with any other information about it. We must realize that insurance adjustors are not appraisers and don't know the value of collectible art and antiques. Art and antiques are complex and value-subjective and, therefore, changing all the time. Insurance companies can handle the house itself and most of its contents, but not the antiques and art: they simply can't know everything. An independent appraiser does not work for your insurance company as adjustors do; they work for *you* and your valuable items. It's not too late to get advice on value now!

After a loss, victims may hire appraisers to provide appraisals (yes, you can order an appraisal *after* a loss) or condition reports, independent of the reports your insurer draws up. When victims present a loss to their insurance company, getting a professional *condition report* for fire, smoke, and water damage to household valuables is key in determining whether to file for their complete replacement cost, or to file for repair/restoration funds. Usually, insurance companies will grant whichever is less. So if the mirror you lost would be cheaper to re-purchase as opposed to an extensive repair, they will offer you a replacement cost, less your deductible. But each policy may be different, especially if you have additional premiums.

Here are some hints about the tried-and-true methods of realizing the value of loss. In some cases, victims can also claim the *loss of value* of an item. So if you owned a Picasso work on paper and, though under glass, it might still have suffered from terrible smoke discoloration, you are still able to claim a loss of value. Say we ascertain it will cost $X to send it down to the Getty Conservation Institute for restoration, but when it's returned, you discover their cleaning process has faded it. The difference between what the Picasso painting was originally worth before the fire, and what it is now worth after the cleaning, is your loss of value.

Another hint: let's say a victim has lost a quite beautiful tureen from a Wedgwood set, but the rest of the 84-piece table setting is fine. The set was complete before the fire, but now one piece will be repaired because we can't find that patterned tureen anywhere. The entire value of the set is now diminished, even if a replacement tureen is found. This depletion of a set after a piece is lost is called *diminution of value* (as opposed to its full replacement cost) and is also claimable.

Here's another valuble tip: some policies have strict limits on what may be paid for items in certain categories: household stuff, silver and gold, jewelry, rugs, electronics, stamps, etc. My policy actually has a limit of $2,500 on jewelry so even if I were to lose $10,000 in jewelry, my insurance would only pay $2,500, less the deductible. The way to cover yourself is to list these specific valuables and to get that confirmed by an appraiser, prior to loss. This is often called an appraisal for replacement cost for the purposes of Rider Coverage.

E.F. called me with an insurance dilemma: a piece of his brother's valuable set of sterling flatware had been stolen. It's not uncommon as the price of silver is currently so high. When his brother claimed it as a loss, he found it wasn't insured for anything close to its true value. Why? Because it wasn't separately scheduled as an appreciable item! Because E.F. had not stated that the silver was an appreciable object, it simply defaulted to depreciable object status.

Think of one's typical homeowner policy that insures depreciable items. Over time, those items will lose their value: for instance, that Herculon sofa which today may be worth only $15 even though your mom paid $2,000 for it in 1987. Unless you have a special rider—a separate policy for appreciable merchandise for which you pay an additional premium covering art and antiques (which increase in value over time)—you may only receive the depreciated value if the item is lost.

Say that a good piece of 18th-century American furniture isn't scheduled separately from your homeowner's policy. Then in a loss situation it might be worth the price paid less 200 years of depreciation. To insure correctly, you will have to pay for rider coverage, but here it's well worth it. The cost to insure a piece of art can range from $.09 to $.20 per $100 of insured value. Then consider that the average homeowner's policy will limit coverage of jewelry and silver to a total of only $2,000. Of

course a good sterling dinner service is worth much more today. So buying that special, appreciable coverage can eliminate the deductible and allow for the fact that art and antiques appreciate over time. If you request a special and more expensive rider coverage, Chubb or Fireman's Fund will increase the insured value up to 50% beyond those limits, if the value has increased at the time of loss. I suggest to my clients that they ask their insurance agent what dollar figure they want to see for scheduled items. Most agents tell me that if an item is worth between $2,000 to $5,000, and it will likely appreciate, one should schedule it on a rider policy.

However, even if you don't have that rider coverage on an average household policy, some items are seen as being in one category by an insurance company and in a total other category by clients. For example, since modern 20th-century furniture has lately increased in value, that Herman Miller modern chair and ottoman set would no longer be classified as household furniture. It would be considered an appreciable collectible even though it doesn't meet the standard for antique classification: 100 years or older. Clients need to understand categories of value

Right: Gauguin, *Fruit on a Table with a Small Dog,* detail, 1889 *(Niccolò)*

and realize the limited knowledge of those who write these policies.

It's amazing how language differs in various contexts and just how much semantics affect insurance policies. A client wrote her sprinklers were on for hours during the California wildfires and her policy states water damage is covered as an unavoidable response to disaster. But water damage is not covered over time, so the mold and split furniture she found three days later may not be covered.

Here's an example from my own policy: without rider coverage or an additional premium, it doesn't cover rare works of art. I have a Chagall print of which 350 had been struck. One can still purchase an edition at auction and, even though that piece is worth over $2,500 and was printed in multiples, it is *not* rare. But my policy still considers it a rare work of art. Experts like myself are asked to testify in court when clients are unhappy with their understanding of an insurance policy. Another line in my policy states I'm not covered for material whose value is based upon age or history. What about a Daum glass Venus figure, given to me with no provenance? It's worth $20,000 and is based on Salvador Dalí's historic preoccupation with the mythological Venus.

Finally, victims need to know that they can dispute. Say you're well into the settlement of your art and antiques claim with your insurance adjustor. But you and the insurance company strongly disagree on the exact amount of loss. You or the company can issue a demand in writing for an independent appraisal. Each party will choose its appraiser and then both appraisers together will choose a single, impartial "umpire." Out of court, the appraisers will then argue about the amount of loss. The appraisers may not agree on value. Remember we have three parties arguing: the umpire as well as the two appraisers. A written statement which two of the three agree upon will determine the final amount of loss. The bad news is the insurance company and the client each pay for their respective appraiser, though the cost of hiring the umpire is split. It looks fair on the outside, but it will be expensive and, hopefully, things won't get that far.

As a fire survivor I want to stress that the burden of proof for both ownership and value (and peace of mind) lies with the *insured!*

## BEGINNER'S LUCK AND A HUGE
# FIND

M<small>R. F.</small> OF THE PHILIPPINES IS A TALENTED artist and came into my office with a drawing he'd found in Singapore. The sketch turned out to be a significant maritime work by Ole Johnsen Seboy, a Scandinavian artist of the 18th century! So I immediately emailed Bruun Rasmussen Auctioneers, a Swedish auction house and they instantly responded: they wanted to auction the drawing with an estimate of 14,000 Danish kroner. So that means the top of the auction house's estimate range is around $2,000. Speculating about just how the 18th-century drawing of a Danish ship was purchased by a Filipino artist in Singapore and then brought to Santa Barbara is useless. The point of the story is that a work of art's journey is often a bit of a fairy tale. This case study emphasizes that *the stranger the provenance, the more likely the story is genuine (at least in part)*.

I'm devoting this chapter to finding artwork in strange places. It does

*Gauguin's picture, together wi[th]
one of Pierre Bonnard's, was s[to]
len in 1961 in London and rea
covered in Italy in 2014.*

occasionally happen, though less than many of you might like to think. Reality TV has taught us that we can open any abandoned storage locker and find a treasure. I put the odds of something like this at a million-to-one. Generally, the more you search, the better you get at sniffing out real finds. Still, I have seen again and again pure beginner's luck, or as some say, the fresh eye is the beginner's eye.

Here's a great example of a true beginner striking it big. An auto factory worker who lived in Turin retired in Sicily in the late 1950s. He took all his possessions and family with him. When the old man died, his son found out that the painting he'd been gazing at in his dad's kitchen for the past 40 years was a true Gauguin! The Italian Culture Minister Dario Franceschini claimed the deceased worker not only had the Gauguin, but also on the very same kitchen wall hung a pricey oil by Pierre Bonnard. Gauguin's is entitled *Fruit on a Table with a Small Dog* (1889) and Bonnard's (1867–1947) is *Woman with Two Armchairs*. Italian authorities estimated both paintings together to be worth between $14 and $40 million.

After the factory worker died, his son hired an appraiser in Sicily to evaluate the paintings. Appraisers often smell something valuable, so our ethical instincts prompt us to contact the invaluable London-based Art Loss Register if we smell shaky provenance. Check the site if you have had art stolen or are on the verge of buying something of value. Since auto line workers generally can't afford true museum-quality Gauguins nor Bonnards, something smelled off. And, after assessing the painting, the Italian appraiser contacted the famed and expert Carabinieri Art Theft Squad. These guys are the bomb: they don't fool around and have been trained by the best undercover mafiosi (hah)!

These Carabinieri discovered the paintings were sold to that factory worker in Turin 40 years ago at an auction for abandoned train items. He'd paid about $100 for both paintings, had them framed and hung in his modest kitchen, without ever knowing the artists' names—and unaware they had been stolen in 1970 from the home of a British collector. The thieves had managed to pose as burglar alarm mechanics and entered the British manor accompanied by imposter policemen. After distracting the cook on duty, they then cut the invaluable paintings from their frames.

Both the Gauguin and Bonnard works were tracked from England to Paris but then the trail went cold. After the paintings had traveled by train from Paris to Turin they were promptly placed in an Italian lost and found. Absolutely no one claimed them and the railroad hadn't any idea of what they had. They were then auctioned off and the Fiat factory worker won them. Some confusion still reigns, as the original owner in London passed away with not a single heir. The son of the Fiat worker claimed ownership but Italian authorities are still figuring out who gets the Gauguin and the Bonnard. Odds are, the Fiat worker's son will own the $30 million in paintings.

Art theft is handled far differently in Europe than in the U.S., especially in a case involving more than one European claim.

But as in Mr. F.'s story, an 18th-century Danish drawing made its way to Singapore and then all the way to Santa Barbara: that's an astonishing example of beginner's luck. The moral of the story is to assume the best until otherwise informed.

Unlikely stories of art traveling across borders are frequently true, and the subject of both court cases and beginner's luck stories. Gold is out there so trust your (in-training) gut instincts.

**Italian carabiniere** *(Georges Jansoon)*

## HOW TO GET RID OF

# THINGS

T HIS TOPIC IS NOT AS EASY TO ADDRESS
as it might seem, especially when you consider that not all items should just
go to eBay. This case study addresses internet research and sales. J.S.'s situation was that she owned a good Pacific Islands painting, which a relative had
collected on a holiday back in the 1950s or 1960s. Should this painting be
listed on eBay?

I say no, and the reason is that eBay's reach is too broad for such a piece.
J.S.'s painting is in a folksy, island genre. It's by a semi-famous artist in that
region, so the percentage of people who collect that narrow style, or that
rather obscure artist, is low and won't sort through millions of eBay listings for it. There are serious collectors out there but they will not trust the
descriptions on eBay. That isn't because they think sellers are being dishonest,
but because they know (it's true) that most eBay sellers are not particularly
knowledgeable about art.

Top-end, high-paying collectors stay away from eBay and similar venues, and collectors of regional styles look for paintings and furniture predominantly in the region of their interest. Moreover, if you as the seller compare a million mediocre offers with offers from two top collectors of that particular genre, you'll get the highest price generated by two top warring collectors. To sell off of a regional painting, contact a dealer in the area who specializes in that region and sell it directly to the gallery, or ask to have it put on consignment at the gallery. Otherwise, sell the artwork in an auction house of that region.

Use AskART.com to get the clues: search for your artist and then go to the Dealers page and shop your painting around to those listed. An example of a regional style is the California coastal plein air paintings, those paintings done in the open air of the Pacific, the coastal mountains, or coastal stands of eucalyptus trees. These were done around the first quarter of the 20th century and one of the best places to sell that genre is in Santa Barbara, California. Santa Barbara has several dealers, such as Frank Goss, plus many active collectors of these pieces. It makes sense that such pieces will do better in Santa Barbara than in, say, New

Jersey, so maximize value by targeting your market. Be aware that if you do sell to a dealer, you'll typically receive 50 to 70% of the retail price, with the rest going to the dealer as a consignment fee.

You can always try auction houses, which typically take a 20% cut, but beware, as most regional auction houses have no bottom end. That means that if and when your piece sells, it may sell for under the auction house estimate (which may be greatly under value). But I do urge everyone to attend at least one auction to see human nature in action!

Here's a final word to the wise about selling online. One client excitedly informed me that new cameras and smartphones have a GPS capability. When you post a picture of one of these on eBay, Craigslist, Facebook, etc., the picture displays a code which tells everyone (including thieves) the location where the picture was taken. This is called "geotagging" and can be quite risky if you have priceless silver or art in your home. Whose idea was that one?

J.S. had a second question about silver which I want to address. She wanted to know if she should dig a hole in her backyard to hide her sterling flatware service because she had noticed that the price of silver was going up, then down, and then up really high. Actually at present it is higher than expected. So should she wait and leave it buried until the market at least levels out? Actually, this is not as silly as it sounds.

Recently I guided a sale of some wonderful silver that had been in a family since 1908. It was a good, heavy, flatware service. We tagged it onto a pickup of some old family paintings that were going to an auction house.

"Tagging" means that we told the auctioneer he could have what he came for if he took the sterling as well. The auctioneer who collected those items relayed that these days he watches his audience as they consider buying silver. He has seen them with their calculators out and they have the catalogue information stating the troy ounce weight. As the bidding increases, they stop raising their paddles because, at some point, it's not worth it to melt it down, even at $38 an ounce. Here's the rub: the value of melted silver was so great in 2010, this auctioneer told me most of the silver goes to the smelters.

Now is the time to think about 20 years from now: will there even be good antique silver hollowware and flatware? There will be little collectible silver left and it will again be sought after, but by then people will want its fine artistry. So maybe J.S. does need to bury that silver for 20 years. The best way to deal with silver is not to sell in this market, unless you really need to.

In a market with a high price for silver, dealers can get away with scalping sellers because so many people think that with the price of silver so high, it's a good time to sell. Actually, more inventory means less money paid for it. And good antique silver which made it through the meltdown years of 2010-11 is, in 2016, infrequently auctioned because there's less of it.

Let's speak about furniture and how to target potential buyers as well as how to offset the cost of delivery with heavy items. I have a client who has a huge, antique French provincial oak armoire. It's truly beautiful but if she doesn't sell it locally, she'll lose money on shipping. Probably the best way to sell is on her local Craigslist or even low-tech bulletin boards. And place flyers with the item's image in offices, clubs, coffeehouses, schools, and church bulletins. Household furniture is typically best sold locally as your core market is right there.

If it's a truly better quality piece of furniture (an armoire that's antique and worth shipping costs) try LiveAuctioneers.com. I usually rely on local dealers and local auction houses to reduce shipping costs.

Or I use Abell Auction Company in Los Angeles and John Moran Auctioneers in Pasadena.

John Moran Auctioneers is onto something good, with its great Discovery Auction. It holds a special sale night for young couples and those new to auctions who may not be up to buying a Picasso but want to furnish their homes with unique items. This auction is a low-key and nonaggressive affair, without high-end items. It's targeted as a bunnyhill for those who may not want the best piece of American 18th-century furniture but still want to collect a good piece.

How and where does one find something's value? Let's say you list an item on an Internet site or approach a gallery or dealer and don't want to ask for my help. I've been collecting for more than 30 years and have a massive private database. If I didn't have my own database, here's how I'd research value. First, look for something unusual about the item. Does yours have any stampings, distinct hallmarks, specific china marks, artist's signatures, or anything else which stands out? If so, research those online and describe the item using the proper terminology. Go to those sites which report what your

type of item sold for. You want to establish the actual value, not what you wish to sell for.

Auction Results on eBay is good for pricing. Some specialty auction houses also report on sale prices, as do the biggies like Christie's and Sotheby's. Go to one of the sites offering pricing guidance (you must pay for this information). I do like WorthPoint.com and also Prices4Antiques.com. Both will feature a photo with the descriptive text. Kovels.com puts out a low-cost Antiques and Collectible Price Guide each year. At least one can ascertain an item's worth and understand its market pricing. Be sure to research online as well as ask an expert to have a look. Your item may be a good copy, reproduction, or giclée (computer-generated artwork). Or an oil or watercolor copy with an exact resemblance to the original (think of the paintings of Thomas Kinkade). Now it's time to consult individuals about what you have.

Broaden your research to include flea market dealers who traffick in your material, and dealers at specialty shows such as the *Santa Barbara Quilt Show*. Why ask more than one? Because a dealer is a dealer and they may want your piece. Dealers may not be 100% honest unless their fellow dealers are nearby—and

Above: Theodor Hoffbauer, Tuilieres Palace

pretending not to listen to one another. While I'm on this topic, dealers are not appraisers! If someone states he or she is an appraiser and then buys the item, that person is not an appraiser. Certified appraisers are not permitted to purchase an item they appraise. Many auction houses try to be sneaky and offer free appraisals to snag a future commission. So just approaching one house does not give you a true reflection of value if the house desires your item. But asking at least three houses will give you a sense of how coveted the item truly is. The same is true of a dealer who wants your item. You get a sense of the item's value if you ask a number of dealers and it will help determine the venue by which to sell your item. If you research the amount something sold for and ask specialty dealers, you'll then get a sense of which auction house sells what and which dealer is interested in what. You may even hear about private collectors who pay close to retail. I have a client who pays over retail for his collectible of choice (and likely would sell his grandmother for it).

Finally, sometimes it pays to give away an item because you can then take the fair market value of it against your taxes. Before you do this, call me or another appraiser as there are many IRS rules on this. I'll give you just one example: in Santa Barbara one can't sell 18th- or 19th-century English antique furniture. Santa Barbara prefers Spanish colonial furniture. It's too expensive to ship English antique furniture to the southeast coast where it sells so much better, and you're far better off just donating. When you do donate, an appraiser will take a national modal value. So, for someone in Santa Barbara who wants to sell English antique furniture, it may pay to donate and take the value against the gross.

We've now covered getting rid of things intelligently. In the long run, ask yourself what an hour of your time is worth. If your item will sell for less than the hours spent selling it, it isn't enough, so donate it!

## APPRAISER-ESE AND TERMS OF THE

# TRADE

Here's a crucial chapter to add to your bargain hunter's notebook! This case study clarifies the *art and antique terminology which all auction houses, dealers, and experts employ*. It should also be helpful when reading estate sale ads or online listings. And do hang around till the end of this chapter when I divulge my favorite techniques for determining which sales are worth attending. Hint: it's all in the wording of the listing.

Many of my clients tell me their chair/dresser/headboard is hand-carved. Unless the piece is pre-1840, this is unlikely. Most elements of furniture which appear hand-carved are generally applied: usually glued or nailed on in strips and then carved with a machine called a spindle carver. The equipment has multiple cutting heads to make many while executing the one. If a piece lacks depth and crispness, you'll know it was machined.

The phrase "period piece" means the piece is from the period in which the style was originally popular. A period piece Chippendale chair would probably date from the mid-18th century to the first quarter of the 19th century, but in rural areas the dates of pieces are *later*. If it's a country Chippendale piece, "by the first quarter of the 19th century" means it was interpreted in the rural areas of England in the manner of the great homes of the 18th century.

So by the time those farmers interpreted the Chippendale style, it was the early 19th century. We can also claim that a mid-century modern chair is a period piece. While modern, clean lines hit the market in the 1920s, that style stayed popular up until the 1960s. Everything can be a period piece and the term doesn't necessarily mean it's either rare or old. In both art and furniture realms, the term "in the style of" signifies that the work resembles the art of a well-known painter or, if furniture, a piece from a well-known period. Today, a buyer can go into any furniture store and buy a so-called "Chippendale" chair but it's after the Thomas Chippendale style (1718–1779). Its aesthetic elements are true to the period in which the designs were created.

I credit Mr. Fred Taylor, writer for WorthPoint.com, for the five "F"

terms of furniture: *Fit, Fittings, Function, Frame,* and *Finish. Fit* implies all the elements fit together and form a pleasing sense of scale (rather than a fat man with a tiny hat, jarringly out of proportion).

*Fittings* relate to hardware: glass, moldings, and the carvings which should be original and in harmony with the piece. *Function* is fairly obvious: does the dresser work? Do the drawers slide and does the chair support one or is it a "breakaway"? *Frame* refers to the architecture of the piece. Does it stand alone and remain solid when stripped down to bare bones? If the drawers are all taken out, is it still a handsome piece? A good item of furniture, like a great artistic composition, should need nothing added. Conversely, it can't sustain itself if anything is taken away.

*Finish,* of course, refers to the varnish, wax, and shellac and must reflect the exact period of the piece. Also note that old finish has a reflective depth to it. Finally, here's my hint for reading a sale ad. If the ad uses the above terms in an unsophisticated or odd way, it's an indication you may be dealing with a rube, a seller who doesn't know what they have. So either the piece will be a disappointment and just an average dog, or you may indeed be onto something. Their poor research may be your gain.

## WHAT'S HOT AND WEIRD AT

# AUCTION

THIS CASE STUDY IS MY LIST OF ODDITIES which some unconventional individuals collect. Just think, for $17,495 you could've purchased a nearly 16 foot long, Edwardian (1840) stuffed crocodile reposing in a beautiful glass and mahogany case and perched on wheels, from Christie's of South Kensington. If you're the lucky owner, please call me because I want to imagine you wheeling the croc around your house or possibly using it for a coffee table. Actually, this stuffed almost 16-foot crocodile on wheels is a rather mild example.

If you missed that one at auction, you can wait for the croc *Utan* to meet his maker and get stuffed. Presently, he's the largest captive croc alive, living in a private collection in South Carolina, at 20 feet long and weighing in over a ton. He can run on his belly up to seven miles per hour and may live to be 130 years old. Personally, I feel there are some things too dangerous to collect and advise readers to stick to paintings and furniture. They won't eat you, generally speaking.

Did you know that an auction record was set back in 2010 at Sotheby's with a sale of $103.7 million? This was the big price paid for Alberto Giacometti's 1961 skinny *Walking Man I*, a six foot tall bronze casting. You may have seen very similar sculptures of the bronze selling for over $100 million. That is because it has *nine* identical brothers. I've only seen two brothers: one was at the Art Institute of Chicago, and another one at Washington's National Gallery.

Who actually bought the sculpture? It was, of course, a big bank: Commerzbank. Banks are big collectors of art because it holds value. How did Giacometti learn to cast bronze? His younger brother Diego created coffee tables and lamps in bronze for some high-end decorators in France in the 1930s. Recently two Diego Giacometti lamps were auctioned off for $98,450 and $89,500, as well as a coffee table at $161,105. That's what's in a famous name—celebrity artists (and their brothers) sell.

Another lucrative sculpture sale occurred: the lifesize *Peter Pan with Pipe* which many have seen at London's Kensington Gardens.

You might recall taking Peter's picture as he's standing on a tree trunk with small forest animals at his feet. The sculptor, Sir George Frampton, realized how popular this big sculpture was becoming and then produced a smaller, 20-inch version of the *Boy Who Would Never Grow Up*. This smaller one sold for $46,495.

Here is a great story about that Peter Pan sculpture: in the 1912 May Day issue of *The London Times*, J.M. Barrie, the famous *Peter Pan* author, asked children to come to Kensington Gardens for a surprise. Overnight, Barrie and his crew had secretly anchored and raised the

life-sized sculpture by Sir George Frampton, to the joy of countless children. The inspiration for the sculpture was Barrie's young friend Michael Llewellyn-Davies, and, although London at first objected to what was perceived as Barrie's naked self-promotion, this lovely *Peter Pan* came to be so admired that it was reproduced in various parks in many English-speaking countries.

In tracking the more unusual items collected, I found an extraordinary family of truly unusual instruments called Stroviols (manufactured by August Stroh in the 1920s). What is a Stroviol, then? Picture a bass viola with strings and frets attached to a huge tin, amplifying horn. Sound is produced on strings and amplified by the horn so that the instrument needs no sound box (as a guitar or violin would). Stroviols were popular oddities in 1920 music halls and, though expensive, were played loudly at home. There are some similar phono-fiddles and phono-mando-lins which may be plucked, bowed, or blown. One sold for $3,580 in March, 2010.

Finally, one of my clients asked me to comment on the latest trends in the porcelain market, leading me to perhaps the greatest oddity. She wrote that her mother's Haviland dinner service was appraised for $800 about 10 years ago, and she was amazed at the current value—only $200 to $300! Art and antiques have taken a big hit in this unstable economy, and polarization of price points is quite evident. There is scant action in items worth $500 or less, but sales at the top 15% of the market are strong, and the prices sharply rising.

It's true that not one collector is filling out their collection today if they are worried about a mortgage. I predict there's a new day coming for art and antiques. But not for fine china (the special event set your mom used).

You can't put that china (some trimmed with gold or silver) in a dishwasher so there's no hope for service porcelain.

To me, it's the biggest oddity of all; now dishwasher ease trumps beauty and history. If you have space, hang on to that china as the rule of rarity will play out in the future. The odds are your childen don't want your formal china tableware. Kids like mine sell off their parents' china for peanuts, and the rarity factor of complete sets will go up, resulting in higher future value.

# INVESTMENTS: THE BEST AND THE

# WORST

I WAS SO HONORED WHEN A REPORTER from *Bloomberg Businessweek* interviewed me about the best and worst art, furniture, and collectible objects to purchase (as well as those not to) for investment. Following that, a reporter from Philadelphia who drafted a story for the website *Investopedia* asked me the same question. So I will divulge: *this case study highlights the best and worst collections owned by my clients.*

The number one worst area in which to invest are those horrifying, over-dressed, limited-edition dolls produced for adults. How horrifying! I received a frantic call from a client in Los Angeles asking me how the heck to sell an entire household full of them—over 2,000 dolls! I had to tell the client it was impossible. Although the dolls might have cost $200 or $300 new, absolutely *no one* will buy them today. This is not the case for antique dolls, which *do* sell. High-end doll collectors sneer at modern dolls because of their abundance. No matter how many eons you hang on to them, no one will buy on the secondary market.

An attorney client of mine was charged with disposing of an older woman's estate and she was just such a modern doll collector. The photos were nightmarish: all sinks, cabinets, and crannies were stuffed with little humanoids. I exhorted him: "Tell your client these will never sell!" Neither, by the way, will the *contemporary* Barbie and Ken dolls (the Surfer, etc.). They remain forever unsalable.

The second worst area is collector plates and no matter what *Bradford Exchange* may claim, they are not salable and will be buried with you! No matter how complete, your series has no resale value. All those cozy English cottages by artist Thomas Kinkade (the Stars of Broadway, the Great Fairytales, or any of the others) are all in garages. In an article entitled "How to Spend It," *The Financial Times* reported that those 1970s and 1980s plates simply cannot be sold. And *The Times* suggested if you're stuck with a collection, one solution might be to hang them in unusual patterns on your own wall: "Clever placement will create a modern-looking wall decoration." I say no matter how clever you are, this will not fly. These plates are dogs and I suggest a Greek dinner with a plate smash to follow!

The third worst area in which to invest is furniture that has a definite style, but is poorly constructed. Do you remember "shabby chic?" Such distressed, wretched furniture is only a compliment to half-dead roses and Victorian hats nailed to the wall. You can't give those pieces away to a thrift store. And remember the 1980s craze for the "Southwestern"? I have seen hideous bedsteads carved out of bleached logs: this furniture is so undesirable it will not even burn!

On a more positive note, here are the three *best* things to purchase in the art and collectibles market and they may surprise you.

Although electronics are now obsolete the day after you purchase them, old electronic technology—that which was in the vanguard and the first of its kind—is hot. For example, there's the brain of the world's first computer, the ENIAC (Electronic Numerical Integrator and Computer), which sold for about $79,500.

The 1949 paper advertising graphics for the Remington Rand Univac computer (the first room-sized, card-eating metal box computer) were estimated to sell for $2,000 to $3,000. An interesting detail is that the first purchaser of the Univac was the IRS. As another example of the lucrative value of technology firsts, I point to the Regina Corona self-changing

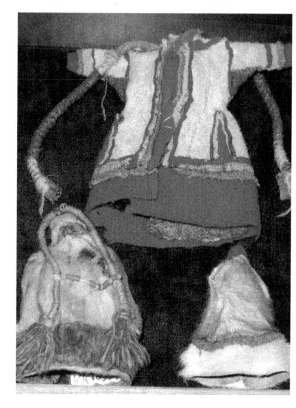

music box (1890–1910) which sold for $25,300.

Remember bedside alarm clocks with flip cards creating numerals? A first edition will eventually be worth something. Every generation has its own period of nostalgia: today's 20-somethings are avid for old vinyl LP records and old Super 8 film cameras.

The second best thing to purchase is paper ephemera: graphics done without the aid of computers. Hand-drawn maps and album covers are fast going the way of last week's fish wrappers, and will be irreplaceable. Printed work created by movable, square metal (hot type) is increasingly rare; the technique is a lost art and not to be replicated. "Ephemera" is an accurate term: it's Greek meaning "lasting only a short time."

The third best area of investment would be native, such as, Hawaiian, American, Aboriginal, and Inuit. But no ivory, feathered, or dug-up items from graves (those will land you in jail)! Native anything is limited because most of these items were created so long ago. Even though prices are still high, they will climb even further due to their rarity. I'd collected arrowhead points for my son for 20 years and am thrilled I did so. Now I only wish I hadn't sold an original stone mortar and pestle

which actually weighed 75 lbs!

The most desirable native material is the period prior to the time of Western influence on native ways. A native art collector must have years of education in order to spot a good item and the genuine article is hard to find. I picked up a superb Native American basket at a thrift store for only six dollars, and it turned out to be worth $800.

Today's most successful collector is half computer electronic nerd and half scholar. Especially hot if also an expert in rare 1970s-80s sound systems: turntables, receivers, and speakers. The market is hungry for these and some of the most chi-chi hotels offer vintage turntables and vinyl records in their most expensive suites.

## SELLING AT AUCTION: 10 GREAT
# STORIES

CHRISTIE'S AND SOTHEBY'S VIEW OF TOP
auction items each year always lead to great personal stories. This case study
shares *the best of them in order of increasing "wow" value.*

This one comes in at 10th place: the family who owned a rare American
Chippendale block-and-shell carved dressing table knew their piece was
worth around $900,000. They knew because in 2005 they had bought it for
that amount, and they also knew that in 1765 a famous American wood-
worker John Goddard had carved it. But times were hard, so they offered it
at auction in January 2010. The great news was that it sold at $5.7 million.
Nice profit, and it demonstrates that good 18th-century American furniture
is still hot.

In ninth place is the case of a retired chocolate factory (Cadbury, Ltd.)
worker from Dorchester, England, who wandered into his local auction
house with an old vase in a box. Lo and behold, it was a 16th-century Ming.
He took home $1.6 million—not a bad retirement bonus!

In eighth place is the jug used for old Benjamin Herington's ashes. This man's ashes had been removed from this gaily-decorated, double-handled, stoneware jug and the jug had been taken to Crocker Farm Auction in Sparks, Maryland. That seller walked out with $138,000. The old folk potter had drowned in Maryland in 1823, and someone had found the jug in an abandoned California closet, dumped the ashes, and sold!

Seventh place goes to a Wayne Gretzky rookie card depicting Gretzky with the Edmonton Oilers. That mint condition card sold for $94,000. Items which were once worth little can accrue great value and, conversely, something once worth a lot may plummet. No one is old enough to remember *The Yellow Kid*, but the comic strip character was so popular in the 1890s that both Joseph Pulitzer's and William Randolph Hearst's newspapers entered a bidding war for the rights. Someone in 2005 bought a comic book of *The Yellow Kid* for $16,800 and sold it in May, 2010, for an unfortunate $1,673. Check out your old comic books: Spiderman's *Amazing Fantasy #15* (1962) sold privately in 2010 for $1.1 million. Have any old comics in your garage?

The next item takes sixth place.

The Chinese, who seem to have oodles of cash these days, are buying Asian items. A savvy Taiwanese snatched up a six-inch oval jade plaque for $94,800 in April, 2010. And an astute Chinese national purchased the contents of a retired Florida couple's closet containing six pieces of antique jade, a censor, teapot, ram figure, and ship carving for $100,000. If you have pre-1950 jade items, call me immediately. Old jade can be quite valuable in today's market.

Sharing fifth place are some items found in two mansions. In Santa Barbara I appraised the contents of a George Washington Smith house and hiding in plain sight were four gorgeous matching ceramic garden fixtures worth $10,000. California ceramics of the early 20th century are great moneymakers.

The second appraisal was for a European mansion with a fountain and a life-size bronze Atlas figure (with the world on his shoulders). This amazing piece was dragged to Sotheby's and it turned out to be a 300-year-old masterwork by Dutch sculptor Adriaen de Vries worth $11 million.

In fourth place are three antique cars, including the world's oldest running car, a 1884 French steam-powered auto, the De Dion-Bouton

et Trepardoux which sold in Hershey, Pennsylvania for a cool $4.6 million. And the second one is actually a transparent auto called the Ghost Car, made for the 1939–1940 New York World's Fair to show the crowds all its interior mechanics. The great 1939 Pontiac Deluxe was a gangsta car if there ever was one and sold for $380,000. Condition in antique cars is everything, unless the car is one of a kind.

Third place goes to the only known authentic photo of Billy the Kid, which sold for $2.3 million to the Koch oil and gas family. Why Mr. Koch treasures this awful looking young man is beyond me. Billy reputedly killed 21 people, including a sheriff, for which he was sentenced to hang in 1878.

Billy escaped for three years, but Sheriff Pat Garrett shot him dead in 1881. The tintype was a personal gift from Billy to Dan Dedrick, one of his henchmen! The photo had been in the Dedrick family since it was first gifted and it's authentic. He was one ugly, skinny kid—I mean Billy, not Mr. Dedrick, whose relative is now $2.3 million richer.

Second place? That goes to a client couple who live in Hope Ranch, near Santa Barbara. They had large, 16th-century majolica wall platters from Urbino, Italy. The three ceramic dishes sold to a Parisian collector for $157,000.

Elizabeth Taylor, adept at getting both men and jewels, had seen La Peregrina when Sotheby's bought it in 1969. Interestingly, Richard Burton outbid the Spanish Royal Family, who had desperately wanted the royal pearl returned after it had been abroad 500 years.

Richard won the Sotheby's auction and presented it as a Valentine's Day gift at Las Vegas's Caesar's Palace while they were both in bed. In *Elizabeth Taylor: My Love Affair with Jewelry*, Taylor wrote she reached down for the pearl "later" (we don't have to ask later than what) only to find it was missing from the setting.

She searched everywhere, refusing to tell why she was crawling around, but found no pearl! Later while playing with her other Valentine's gift, a puppy, she opened its mouth and there was La Peregrina—fortunately unswallowed.

My advice to collectors is to attend a few auctions. They are the one true social arbiter of value.

## COLLECTOR TO CONNOISSEUR:

# ENTRÉE

W HEN I WAS TEACHING DECORATIVE
Arts at a California city college in the 1990s, I had a room full of
English-speaking students and one Japanese student,
Haruto. I wasn't worried about him understanding my
classes, because most lectures were illustrated with
slides (you remember slides?). Yet, Haruto found it
difficult to grasp my lectures about the 1960s aesthetic,
especially psychedelic forms of pop and poster art. I'd
driven my son's 1969 orange Chevy Camaro Super-
Sport to school that evening, so during the break I
took young Haruto out to the parking lot. It struck me
that the car would also make a great teaching tool on
the art of the '60s.

Every person's aesthetic, like every era's pieces, has a

certain shape. You see how someone responds to and collects certain ones. I've seen countless homes over 26 years and recognize the shape of a person's style. This case study *elucidates connoiseurship.*

How do I know when someone has the eye? D.M.'s house is a perfect little gem set amid a lovely, well-manicured garden flourishing with vines and flowers. The small interior of the house spoke of D.M.'s delicate and flowing linear aesthetic. It's organic yet simple, and in the winter, the colors are set off by intense white, blue, and silver. D.M. knew exactly what he liked, so everything—no matter how eclectic—fit together. Some master designers say "It is what you leave out that matters." D.M. had selected only specific areas of his collection to showcase. Some of what surrounded me included native Inuit sculpture, 18th-century British pottery, contemporary Canadian painters, Chinese celadon, 18th-century Brown furniture, bamboo seating from the hip 1950s, and Quimper faience (glazed ceramics). How can some people pull this off? Simply because they know the "shape" of their style and stick to it.

He had not only created flow in that tiny house, but he'd also purchased his lovely items at a time when Canadian artists were inexpensive since they were considered regional. Moreover, his objects of Canadian native and realist art were also exceptionally well-crafted. His purchases were of top quality, informed by his eye.

Part of the purpose of my visit was to help D.M. find buyers for items he'd deemed unworthy and which he'd relegated to the garage. D.M. had graduated to a connoisseur. When someone disposes of the bottom-third of their collection, they may be crowned with the connoisseur's tiara. They have begun to distill their collection.

It means that they arrived at a "shape" of style and they trace that arc in their collecting. This is how a connoisseur differs from a collector: when you know your shape, everything you love works together to enhance it.

Think of very different objects you love. What shape do they share? Group together just three of those things and study their commonality to discover your shape. Once you recognize it, stick to it.

Think of someone you love, for whom you always find the right gift: you know that person's shape. Practice this shape recognition in your own home by training your eye, and you'll have achieved the rank of true connoisseur.

## THE GREAT AMERICAN SELL-OFF:

# BOOMERS

A LOT OF NEWS LATELY DEALS WITH MY Baby Boomer generation. I've determined a trend: Boomers wish to simplify their material lives. Maybe you yourself have wondered, as I have, if anyone really wants their stuff. This case study *covers disposal, liquidating and paring down—purging*.

Seventy-six million Americans were born between 1946 and 1964. We now control 80% of the personal financial assets and more than 50% of discretionary spending power *and* are responsible for more than half of consumer spending. We grew up under the microscope of consumer marketing experts wanting us to buy, buy, buy! And we obliged.

We've been gathering stuff and amassing clutter: at least one in 10 have a full, off-site, rented storage unit. This was unheard of 30 or 40 years ago. We were born into the great days of the postwar boom, a time when keeping up with the Joneses meant more TVs, cars, phones, clothes, boats, and revolving furniture. And don't forget, we bought retail without credit cards.

Now my generation has become empty nesters and we scan our homes, garages, and storage units wondering just how we got so much *stuff*. Business journals report that in the last five years, boomers have shied away from long-term estate planning. Is this because we don't really believe we're getting old? After all, 50 is the new 30, right? We don't want to think about who is going to have to sell all our stuff someday. Denial is a wonderful thing!

But 10,000 people will turn 65 today and then about 10,000 more will cross that same threshold everyday for the next 19 years. So those of us reaching 50 are now thinking of the Big Purge. We want to simplify and clear a new path to becoming unstuck. Boomers have way too much stuff, but the problem is that the market is not only cramped, it's also underfunded. No one wants what Boomers wanted when they bought. In the past decade, we've spent nearly $2 trillion annually on household and consumer goods. Our stuff is truly problematic and my clients tell me how impossible it is to

find buyers. They've tried eBay and Craigslist, hired estate sale outfits, called auction houses—and still, there's much to donate.

The value of standard American furniture from the typical middle-class Boomer era is way down, at least 50% from when it was purchased. Disposable household goods aren't only our problem: the EPA reports 23% more household stuff is in dumps and landfills than in 2000. Think about the electronics in your home that are almost obsolete. We have twice as many unused electronics as in 2007. Then think about all the hazardous stuff tossed into our landfills. Jewelry is hard to sell unless it's gold or silver and wristwatch sales are down by 28% on eBay from 2008 to 2010, since time is on cell phones now. And middle range $2,000 to $10,000 fine art at auction fell 43% from 2008 to 2010.

The good news is that the average thrift store has tripled donations. Have you noticed the sheer size of some Goodwill shops? Have you seen the one in the International District of Seattle? It's a megamall of stuff and is now wisely making room for more. If you try to downsize and can't afford to donate, my advice is to approach the specialty auction houses (small ones) or else specialty dealers. Do a search to find out who buys and who auctions what *you* have. As an example, R.O. Schmitt Fine Arts only auctions clocks.

For art pottery, I send items to David Rago Auctions, which handles art pottery, art glass, and craftsmen-era stuff. For mid-century art and furniture, I turn to dealers in Palm Springs, California, or to Los Angeles Modern Auctions (in LA). Often I sell by advertising locally, or using local estate sale staff who work like dogs for a percentage of the sale

price. And sometimes your friends are your best market, so suggest a private wine and cheese event before the hard opening of your estate sale.

I'm always weeding three decades worth from the bottom end: I donate, but giving away stuff with emotional ties is hard. It gets easier as you give more away, and if you move, that load will become a curse. So I have a garage box that's always ready for a Goodwill item.

My rule (which I often disobey) is if one thing comes into the house, something else has to leave.

Apartment of a Hoarder, 2009 *(Grap)*

# A BURNING QUESTION: AM I A

# HOARDER?

MY CLIENT ASKED ME TO ADDRESS HER
deepest fear. She's an avid collector but worried: "Am I a hoarder? Or am I just
a collector? Could I be a hoarder in collector's clothing?" I have, in fact, seen
hoarders' homes and it's clear who they are. This is the difference between a
hoarder's home and a collector's: in a hoarder's the mess is life-threatening
and life-restricting. Their so-called "collection" does not add to the quality of
their lives; rather, it's become a pathological block to it.

I have seen boxes blocking windows, doors, and plumbing and if the
owner is not actively involved in packing to move, I judge those objects have
become a problem and that the owner is a hoarder. This case study deal with
*the hoarder—a label not to be taken lightly*. Collecting is different from hoarding in that the former involves restraint. A collector is discerning. That may
not always be obvious to the collector's friends or family, but collectors do
discriminate about what they do and *don't* want to add.

*Real collectors have the psychological balance to take the hit and learn from loss. Collecting is a lot like life!*

Of course, collecting things is infinitely more problematic in this era of the Internet. The accessibility of objects online, all adorned with lovely images and purchased with just a keystroke to PayPal (paying is a pal?), can be risky. Personally, I don't buy online because I want to see and touch the art or object in person. I've even been known to smell silver and taste oil paint!

A true collector engages in a long process of material research. They are, of course, emotionally involved with their objects, but they are not compelled to buy for nostalgia's sake. They assess an object's place in history, they examine value, the date of creation, who created it and why, its social impact, the material composition, craftsmanship level, etc. The goal of a collector is to know as much as possible about a class of object so that no one knows more than you do at the flea market or auction.

Collectors still feel the excitement of the hunt and can be swept away. But if a mistake ends up in their house the true collector will smile bravely and learn from it (and then get rid of it before a spouse might complain)! They also have *budgets*, and hate to pay top dollar for anything. The exception is if an object is so rare or if it's needed to complete a full set. Then top dollar is what you simply must pay. Collectors do not amass more than one type of object solely because there are identicals. They'll narrow or cull their collection as they learn more about that class. A collector might consider marbles a member of a class of glass objects, and a marble collector will likely focus on just one type of marble.

The ultimate goal of a collector is to become a *connoisseur*, and I know when my clients are on the verge of becoming one. They'll call and instruct me to sell the bottom third of their collection so they can focus on the remaining top two-thirds. Then they'll add to the top instead of acquiring at the bottom end.

The connoisseur's focus is always on increasing knowledge of their specific area. These bona fide connoisseurs know that quality, however it may be perceived, trumps quantity.

I bought a 1960s Bendix Brakes advertising clock in "perfect" condition. One item in perfect condition is of far greater value than 100 in poor condition. Buyer's remorse is a real disease, and if you've collected

## HOW MARBLES ARE MADE.

MOST of the stone marbles used by the boys are made in Germany The refuse only of the marble and agate quarries is employed, and this is treated in such a way that there is practically no waste. Men and boys are employed to break the stone into small cubes, and with their hammers they acquire a marvellous dexterity. The little cubes are then thrown into a mill, consisting of a grooved bedstone and a revolving runner. Water is fed to the mill and the runner is rapidly revolved, while the friction does the rest. In half an hour the mill is stopped, and a bushel or so of the perfectly round marbles taken out. The whole process costs the merest trifle.

A 1901 description of marble manufacture in Germany *(Glenda Green)*

for awhile, you've experienced regret. There are also obsessives who constantly ruminate on "the one that got away." My best collectors hate themselves for this, but move on. I, however, still loathe the woman who grabbed a coveted painting away from me at the thrift store. Collectors must have the psychological balance to take the hit and learn from loss. In other words, collecting is a lot like life!

# NUGGETS
# I NEVER
# SOLD

# IN WHAT I DO, A LOT OF ITEMS MUST BE

sold or donated. I've parted with things I sadly now regret, though many of my favorite antiques are still living at Villa Elizabeth. Some of my pieces have increased greatly in value, much to my surprise, because I buy mainly from thrift stores. Some pieces have increased only in the pleasure they give me. This case study reveals *Elizabeth's Top 10 Keepers, items I never sold and never will.*

- The complete score of Beethoven's *Fidelio* published in Leipzig, Germany, by Breitkopf & Härtel in 1864. Beethoven completed *Fidelio* from 1805 (first version) to 1814 (third version) and my own copy was printed 59 years after its first performance in Vienna. My great uncle had worked in Leipzig's publishing world and he must have snagged an unused copy. I'm unsure of its worth, but a letter by Beethoven to his publisher before he died sold in 2014 for $9,000.
- An English Regency tea caddy box (1800–1820). Each box within the main box is as beautifully painted as the box itself. A true mark of craftsmanship

is seen whenever the non-exposed elements of an object are lovingly "finished."

- A beautiful Chagall lithograph, hand-colored by the master. It was used for a poster to advertise his 1956 gallery opening. I bought it from the wife of a Dutch ambassador who had attended the opening in 1956. I paid too much, but I treasure it and can picture the opening with Chagall's fellow artists. It's worth $5,000 today.

- A turquoise-blue, ceramic flower frog from 1910-1920, featuring a nude Lady of the Lake caressing a swan. It was potted in Colorado by the Van Briggle Company. My grandmother bought it when she and her husband took my dad on a nationwide tour in their Model T. It's worth $500 but invaluable in sentiment. It was the only "nude" in my very religious grandmother's entire household.

- A classic 1950s Chanel black dress with a sheer blouse top and wide, full tea-length skirt, which was once the height of chic. A mouse chewed through the skirt and netting, but I had it restored. It's from Dallas, and I paid $5. If the mice hadn't "altered" it for me, the dress would be worth $1,500.

- A cool hat by the Italian designer Elsa Schiaparelli (that great rival of Coco Chanel). Elsa Schiaparelli had collaborated with Dalí and Giacometti: this creation is a Dalí design for her winter 1937 collection. A tiny hat in black felt, it was Dalí and Schiaparelli's "shoe" hat. Yes, a shoe, worn with toe pointing forward as the brim. Wearing this is ridiculous but I'm in good company. That same year Dalí and Schiaparelli designed a lobster evening gown for Wallis Simpson, the American divorcée who married the Duke of Windsor (in line to be king of England). The hat is worth $1,200.

- I serve myself dinner with an art deco set of German silver flatware created between the World Wars. That is when Germany could only produce a lower silver grade, not sterling. The design is hard-edged with a distinctive gray cast to the silver. I bought it at an estate sale in San Diego, California, for $35, the price of stainless. Why not use your silver every day? This "800" silver ("800" because it's 800 parts silver, versus sterling, which is 925 parts silver) is worth $900 today.

- My formal china never sees the light of day, but features a luscious pattern with large, blooming pink roses. Wedgewood had created the pattern for actress Cyd Charisse. She had taken up ballet early,

(J.Flandrick)

after childhood polio hit her. I'd known her personal secretary and both she and Charisse decorated in an ultra-feminine style (it's mine, as well and I call it "early brothel")! It's worth almost nothing in this market: a gold-edged, handwash-only, porcelain dinner service.

- I love my very ugly yellow Hall pottery teapot from the 1950s Jewel Tea Co. I'd grown up in rural Illinois and a Jewel Tea man would flog a huge basket of household items door-to-door. It was jammed with mesmerizing junk and their autumn leaves pattern was every housewife's dream temptation.

- Finally, every night at dinner, I light a pair of 1890 ecclesiastic (church altar) candelabra. Each are cast in bronze and weigh 20 pounds. The pair is worth $2,000. Since they're huge, I must use extra-large candles, but I love oversized items (strange, as Villa Elizabeth is but a tiny duplex). My son and his fiancée asked for these to be used on the altar at their wedding.

- If you think about what you'd *never* sell, you'll be painting a picture of who you are!

# CONCLUSION: THE LURE OF
# STUFF

SOME OF US ARE JUST STUFF PEOPLE.
I see comrades at flea markets, Alpha Thrift, The Salvation Army, Bargain Box, and Goodwill, and wonder why we buy each others' stuff. What is a flea market (aside from the 19th-century French origination *marchés aux puces*) in terms of desire for more stuff? Check out the book *Stuff: Compulsive Hoarding and the Meaning of Things* by psychiatrists Frost and Steketee. They're the first to study the psychological hold that things can have on people. To some, it's to the point of pathological: does my stuff own me or do I own my stuff? It can become a problem. I've been appraising in people's homes for 30 years and almost every year I encounter at least one hoarder. What is it about StuffPeople that compels us to haunt thrifts and the fleas? What are we looking for?

Dr. Michael Prokopow teaches a course called "Stuff" at Toronto's OCAD University. He was quoted in the *New York Times* of May 15, 2011: "For most people who go on these ritualized scavenger hunts, looking for something that they may not know exists, it is a kind of pilgrim's progress through the detritus of the past." He solemnly explained that those of us who search for Stuff have a mind-set: "Flea markets proliferate a volume of goods needing to be sold and people who are hungry—emotionally and aesthetically—sorting out the meaning of life." (It's me in a nutshell.) Could there be another more positive, nostalgic reason for loving the fleas? Perhaps the economy, or the fact that many StuffPeople are individualists who don't want to dress and decorate like others. We don't want to buy clothes from big-box stores, or banal stripmalls as those avenues are all too predictable and boring. Plus *that* new stuff is limited—not real, glorious junk! We enjoy scavenging with all

> *Flea markets proliferate...goods needing to be sold and people who are hungry—emotionally and aesthetically—to sort out the meaning of life.*
>
> —Dr. Michael Prokopow

its unpredictability and unknowns. There's an allure to the hunt.

Perhaps we are looking for something to enliven us, if not exactly to search out the meaning in one's life.

Thrift and flea market shopping is social, a ritual with others, and unmatched by ordering online. We can assert our individuality in public settings and for that we don't need or want technology.

We may just pine for simpler days when we could discuss items with fellow scavengers. Discovering an object that was almost tossed can feel heroic (we like to rescue things). I saved a pair of men's size 12, white patent-leather, platform disco shoes from Goodwill. I can't wear them, but I saved them. That's nostalgia, not mental illness, don't you think? It's about respecting the lives of Stuff. And my Stuff has lives. My unsigned oil paintings are my "orphans."

I maintain that people neither really use nor need their stuff: they just like having it around. Maybe it triggers a memory. One friend loves old lunchboxes, which echo her childhood. Another collects silk scarves, her only affordable luxury.

Another's passion are old typewriters as a memory of journalism school. A gent collects old vacuum tubes, those antique radio bulbs, harkening back to when radio was the sole entertainment. StuffPeople can say to others "I'm the type of guy who collects old electronics," or "I'm the kind of gal who wears old cowboy boots."

Our Stuff resonates with who we are and sends a message about us. Finally, I love the performance aspect of flea market settings because we're all performing a ritual. I tell myself I'm looking for something no one else has and I don't think about stuff no one else wants (it's too close to the truth perhaps). I tell myself I'll be different after I buy stuff and will wear the difference as a sign of uniqueness. But I also love to donate.

Did I tell you about the yellow vase? An older woman told me that the high point of her life was finding her mother's yellow vase at a flea market. It was a vase her mother had abandoned when fleeing the Nazis. She knew it was her mom's by the unique crack it bore. That's a jolting message about the meaning of Stuff.

May you always be surrounded by objects you cherish and have the time to research them. And may you have the courage to part with them when the time is right.

I TRIED THAT JAPANESE
decluttering trend where you
hold each thing you own and
throw it out if it doesn't give you joy.
So far, I've thrown out all the
vegetables and the electric bill.

# DR. ELIZABETH STEWART, Ph.D.

(Santi Visalli)

Dr. ELIZABETH STEWART IS A 50-YEAR expert on Stuff. A certified member of the Appraisers Association of America, she has spent a lifetime in the world of personal belongings. As a kid in Illinois she ran farm auction sales, as a young woman in San Francisco she traded art and antiques, and as a single mom she sold vast estates from her San Diego warehouse.

A Santa Barbara businesswoman, scholar, and media personality, Elizabeth's doctoral dissertation "The Material Image: Why Collectors Collect" focuses on the psychology of connoisseurs, hoarders, and fetishizers. A 30-year career appraiser, Elizabeth has taught clients and organizations how to create collections, find value and provenance, what to bequeath, and how to donate. She travels with her custom road show. Half socializing, half crash course, this work is a high-spirited ride in the world of what YOU own, as you share the secret files of a seasoned professional at the top of her game.

Front Cover, Title Page, and Page x: *TULIPS*, detail, Jeff Koons. 2015. Photo by Zarateman *[CC0, via Wikimedia Commons]*.

Back Cover: AUTHOR ELIZABETH STEWART. 2016. John Flandrick *[Used with permission]*.

Page vii: *LE CAVALIER ARABE*, Raoul Dufy. 1914. Musée d'Art Moderne de la Ville de Paris *[Public domain-US, via Wikimedia Commons]*.

Page ix: FUNERARY DRESS, King Pakal of Palenque, 7th century, detail. Photo by Wolfgang Sauber. *[GFDL or CC BY-SA 3.0, via Wikimedia Commons]*.

Page xi: TEMPLAR TOWER, detail. 2010. Jack Ma *[GFDL or CC BY-SA 3.0, via Wikimedia Commons]*.

Page xi: ARMOIRIES ROBERT DE SABLÉ. 2008. Odejea *[CC BY-SA 3.0 or GFDL, via Wikimedia Commons]*.

Page xiii: *THE ANNUNCIATION*, detail. Master of the Llangattock Hours *[Public domain, via Wikimedia Commons]*.

Page xiv: *BROWNEA ARIZA*, detail. 2008. Bernard M. *[Public domain, via Wikimedia Commons]*.

Page 1: *GREY AND YELLOW ABSTRACT ART PAINTING*. Gallery T30 *[Used with permission, via Shutterstock]*.

Page 2: *THE SCOUT: FRIENDS OR FOES*, detail, Frederic Remington *[Public domain]*.

Page 3: *AIDING A COMRADE*, detail, Frederic Remington *[Public domain, via Wikimedia Commons]*.

Page 4: *ARIZONA COWBOY*, Frederic Remington *[Public domain, via Wikimedia Commons]*.

Page 7: *LA MADELEINE, PARIS, EVENING STREET SCENE*. Constantin Alexeievitch Korovine. Private Collection of Bill Dutton. Photo by John Flandrick *[Used with permission]*.

Page 8: PAUL REYNARD, 1987. David Heald *[CC BY 3.0, via Wikimedia Commons]*.

Page 8: POSTER FOR THE SALON DES APPAREILS MÉNAGERS. 1924. Published by the French Ministry of Public Education *[Public domain, via Wikimedia Commons]*.

Page 9: ABORIGINAL ROCK ART ON THE BARNETT RIVER, MOUNT ELIZABETH STATION, detail. 2013. Photo by Graeme Churchard *[CC BY 2.0, via Wikimedia Commons]*.

Page 10: MUNGO MAN. Photo by James Maurice Bowler *[CC BY-SA 3.0, via Wikimedia Commons]*.

Page 11: PARIS, GRAND PALAIS. 2011. Photo by Vincent Desjardins *[CC BY 2.0, via Wikimedia Commons]*.

Page 13: *DIE HULDIGUNG*, Wilhelm Camphausen *[Public domain, via Wikimedia Commons]*.

Page 14: *IM PARK DER VILLA D'ESTE*, Carl Blechen. 1830 *[Public domain, via Wikimedia Commons]*.

Page 15: GALLERY IN THE SUN. 2012. DeGrazia Foundation *[Public domain, via Wikimedia Commons].*

PAGE 16: CHAPEL MURAL *[Public domain, via Wikimedia Commons].*

PAGE 17: TED AND DIEGO *[Public domain, via Wikimedia Commons].*

PAGE 18: TED AND MARION DEGRAZIA, detail *[Public domain].*

Page 19: *THE ARNOLFINI WEDDING.* Jan van Eyck *[Public domain, via Wikimedia Commons].*

Page 19: *THE ARNOLFINI WEDDING,* DETAIL OF CONVEX MIRROR. Jan van Eyck *[Public domain, via Wikimedia Commons].*

Page 20: *LAS MENINAS,* detail. Diego Velázquez *[Public domain, via Wikimedia Commons].*

Page 20: *DÜRER, SELF-PORTRAIT,* detail. Albrecht Dürer *[Public domain, via Wikimedia Common].*

Page 21: *REMBRANDT, SELF-PORTRAIT,* detail. 1630. Rembrandt *[Public domain, via Wikimedia Common].*

Page 23: *MADONNA OF THE PINKS.* Raphael *[Public domain, via Wikimedia Commons].*

Page 24: FORGERY OF A GOYA PORTRAIT. Francisco Goya *[Public domain, via Wikimedia Commons].*

Page 26: VICTORIA AND ALBERT MUSEUM - NATIONAL ART LIBRARY. Photo by Wuselig *[Public domain, via Wikimedia Commons].*

Page 27: *LE CAVALIER ARABE,* Raoul Dufy. 1914. Musée d'Art Moderne de la Ville de Paris *[Public domain-US, via Wikimedia Commons].*

Page 30: SALVADOR DALÍ. Roger Higgins, *World Telegram* staff photographer *[Public domain, via Wikimedia Commons].*

Page 32: SALON DU LIVRE ANCIEN ET DE L'ESTAMPE. 2013. Lionel Allorge *[GFDL or CC BY-SA 3.0 or FAL, via Wikimedia Commons].*

Page 33: EMPTY FRAMES AT ISABELLA STEWART GARDNER MUSEUM. 2013. Federal Bureau of Investigation *[Public domain, via Wikimedia Commons].*

Page 35: GHENT ALTARPIECE. Jan van Eyck, circa 1390–1441 *[Public domain, via Wikimedia Commons].*

Page 36: *THE CONCERT.* Johannes Vermeer. *[Public domain, via Wikimedia Commons].*

Page 37: *THE NIGHTWATCH.* Rembrandt. *[Public domain, via Wikimedia Commons].*

Page 39: *PIETÀ* AT SAINT PETER'S BASILICA VATICAN, detail. Michelangelo *[CC0, via Wikimedia Commons].*

Page 41: TURNTABLE, 2013 *[CC0, via Pexels].*

Page 42: HUNGRY, HUNGRY HIPPOS. 2008. Dave Fischer. *[CC BY-SA 2.0, via Wikimedia Commons].*

Page 45: PHILCO PREDICTA TV. John Flandrick. *[Used with permission].*

Page 48: TSD RADIOARCHIV JUKE BOX, detail. Kinsme *[GFDL or CC BY-SA 3.0, via Wikimedia Commons].*

Page 48: VINTAGE SUPERIOR INSTRUMENTS CO. TRANS-CONDUCTANCE VAC-UUM TUBE TESTER, MODEL TV-12, CIRCA 1955, detail. Joe Haupt *[CC BY-SA 2.0, via Wikimedia Commons]*.

Page 49: VIENNA-RATHAUS. 2007. Marek Slusarczyk *[CC BY 3.0, via Wikimedia Commons]*.

Page 51: DRESDEN CHRISTMAS TREE ORNAMENTAL CANDY CONTAINER, SIL-VERED COMPOSITION, GERMANY. 1876-1925. *[Photo used with permission by Michael Bertoia, Bertoia Auctions, 2141 DeMarco Drive, Vineland, NJ 08360, www.bertoiaauctions.com.]*

Page 53: DOLL'S EYE, 2016. Jeltovski *[via Morguefile.com]*.

Page 54: DOLL PORTRAIT, detail. 2015. Evacatrin *[CC BY-SA 4.0, via Wikimedia Commons]*.

Page 56: FRIENDSHIP FOKKER, 2016. *[Photo used with permission by Michael Bertoia, Bertoia Auctions, 2141 DeMarco Drive, Vineland, NJ 08360, www.BertoiaAuctions.com]*.

Page 57: GRASSHOPPER, 1936. *Antique Toy World*.

Page 58: CAST-IRON MOTORCYCLE WITH RIDER. 1925-1935. From the collection of Dr. Frank Seifried, Jr., in honor of his dad Frank (author's grandfather, a St. Louis motorcycle cop). John Flandrick *[Used with permission]*.

Page 59: NAN WALTER. Nancy Seifried *[Used with permission]*.

Page 60: ELIZABETH STEWART, John Flandrick *[Used with permission]*.

Page 61: UNIVERSITÄTSBIBLIOTHEK HEIDELBERG OBERGESCHOSS. 2016. Immanuel Giel *[Public domain, via Wikimedia Commons]*.

Page 62: A RARE FIRST EDITION OF CHARLES DARWIN'S *ON THE ORIGIN OF SPE-CIES*, Treasures Exhibition, Natural History Museum, detail. 2013. John Cummings *[CC BY-SA 3.0, via Wikimedia Commons]*.

Page 64: *BEN FRANKLIN*, detail. Joseph Duplessis. *[Public domain, via Wikimedia Commons]*.

Page 65: *ZUR GESCHICHTE DER KOSTÜME*, 1890. Munich, 2016. Mary Schlesinger *[Used with permission]*.

Page 67: *THE BOOKWORM*. Karl Spitzweg. *[Public domain, via Wikimedia Commons]*.

Page 68: BIBLIO ALEXANDRIA. 2008. Photo by RedTurtle *[Public domain, via Wikimedia Commons]*.

Page 69: BULLE DU PAPE CLÉMENT V SUSPENDANT L'UNION DES BIENS DE L'OR-DRE DU TEMPLE À L'ORDRE DE L'HÔPITAL DANS LES ROYAUMES HISPANIQUES. French National Archives *[Public domain, via Wikimedia Commons]*.

Page 71: THE KNIGHTS TEMPLAR BURNED IN THE PRESENCE OF PHILIP THE FAIR AND HIS COURTIERS, detail. Boucicaut Master Illuminator *[Public domain, via Wikimedia Commons]*.

Page 72: FUNERARY DRESS, King Pakal of Palenque, 7th century, detail. Wolfgang Sauber *[GFDL or CC BY-SA 3.0, via Wikimedia Commons]*.

Page 73: MAYAN-STUCCO PORTRAIT HEAD. Walters Art Museum *[CC BY-SA 3.0 or GFDL, via Wikimedia Commons]*.

Page 75: MAYAN. 2015. Awilix *[CC BY-SA 4.0, via Wikimedia Commons]*.

Page 76: PHARAOH AND TWO HEADS, TWO-SIDED RELIEF. 2011. Daderot *[Public domain, via Wikimedia Commons]*.

Page 77: GREEK BRONZE HELMET. Altes Museum, Berlin. 2014. Anagoria *[GFDL or CC BY 3.0, via Wikimedia Commons]*.

Page 78: NIPPON PORCELAIN BOWL. 2016. Mary Schlesinger *[Used with permission]*.

Page 80: WARWICK CASTLE CIVIL WAR HELMET, detail. 2016. Chris Nyborg *[GFDL, via Wikimedia Commons]*.

Page 82: *PORTRAIT OF CROMWELL*, detail. Hans Holbein the Younger (1497/1498–1543*) [Public domain, via Wikimedia Commons]*.

Page 83: *RETREAT OF NAPOLEON FROM LEIPZIG*, detail. 1813, Louis Dupre. *[Public domain, via Wikimedia Commons]*.

Page 85: OSTTEIL SANSOUCCI, detail. 2015. Suse *[GFDL or CC-BY-SA-3.0, via Wikimedia Commons]*.

Page 86: CARTIER BUILDING IN LISBON, detail. 2013. Elfabso *[CC BY-SA 3.0, via Wikimedia Commons]*.

Page 87: PIERRE CARTIER WITH WIFE AND DAUGHTER, detail. 1926. *Bain News Service* photograph. *Forms part of: George Grantham Bain Collection (Library of Congress). USA DIGITAL ID: cph 3c24396 http://hdl.loc.gov/loc.pnp/cph.3c24396, CAR #: 99472340 [PPOC(1) Copyrighted free use, via Wikimedia Commons]*.

Pages 88-89: 1920's SANTA BARBARA STREETCAR AT A MISSION CANYON LOCATION, detail. 2016. John Flandrick. *[Used with permission]*.

Page 90: GALILEO, detail. Ottavio Leoni *[Public domain, via Wikimedia Commons]*.

Page 90: GALILEO'S FINGER, detail. NASA Blueshift. *[CC BY 2.0, via Wikimedia Commons]*.

Page 92: ROYAL FAMILY ON THE BALCONY, detail. 2011. Magnus D. *[CC BY 2.0, via Wikimedia Commons]*.

Page 93: ROYAL WEDDING CAKE REPLICA. 2016. *[Used with permission, via AmazingCakeIdeas.com]*.

Page 95: SUBMERGED BUGATTI. Donna-Tom Zwart. *[Used with permission]*.

Page 97: EB ETTORE BUGATTI. 2008. Brian Snelson *[CC BY 2.0, via Wikimedia Commons]*.

Page 98: *A COMMANDER BEING ARMED FOR BATTLE*, detail. Peter Paul Rubens. Christie's Images *[Public domain, via Wikimedia Commons]*.

Page 99: SELF-PORTRAIT, detail. Peter Paul Rubens *[Public domain, via Wikimedia Commons]*.

Page 100: GAL IN BARREL, circa 1920. Halsey Photo, Pull-Rak Co. Inc. *[Used with permission]*.

Page 101: TRES TOMBS A SANT ANTONI, detail. 2011. Jordiferrer *[CC BY-SA 3.0, via Wikimedia Commons]*.

Page 102: THE LADY GODIVA PROCESSION. Thomas Stevens, detail, Honolulu Museum of Art. 2015. Photo by Hiart *[CC0, via Wikimedia Commons]*.

Page 103: THOMAS STEVENS, detail. Herbert Art Gallery and Museum, Coventry *[CC BY-SA 3.0, via Wikimedia Commons]*.

Page 104: SÈVRES-FOURS-AMOUR FALCONET BISCUIT, detail. 2013. Photo by Myrabella *[CC BY-SA 4.0, via Wikimedia Commons]*.

Page 105: *THE SWING*, detail. Jean-Honoré Fragonard *[Public domain, via Wikimedia Commons]*.

Page 106: A STATE CHAIR. Illustration by M. Jancowski of York, from *Illustrated History of Furniture, From the Earliest to the Present Time from 1893* by Frederick Litchfield, (1850-1930) *[Public domain, via Wikimedia Commons]*.

Page 108: RELIQUARY BUST OF SAINT CATHERINE OF ALEXANDRIA, ca 1465, Metropolitan Museum of Art, Gift of J. Pierpont Morgan, 1917. *[www.metmuseum.org]*.

Page 109: *RIEMENSCHNEIDER TRAUERNDE FRAUEN*, detail. Tilman Riemenschneider *[Public domain, via Wikimedia Commons]*.

Page 111: *BEIM ANTIQUITÄTENHÄNDLER*. Albert Josef Franke (1860-1924) *[Public domain, via Wikimedia Commons]*.

Page 112: MICROCOSM OF LONDON PLATE 006-AUCTION ROOM, CHRISTIE'S. Thomas Rowlandson (1756–1827) and Augustus Charles Pugin (1762–1832). *[Public domain, via Wikimedia Commons]*.

Page 115: BLACK FINISH ZIPPO LIGHTER. 2015. Jonathan Mauer *[CC BY-SA 4.0, via Wikimedia Commons]*.

Page 116: CHRISTIE'S AUCTION PREVIEW EXHIBITION, detail. Wanchai, Hong Kong. 2012. Sunbeamprowce *[CC BY-SA 3.0, via Wikimedia Commons]*.

Page 118: SOTHEBY'S AUCTIONEER ADRIAN BIDDELL, detail. 2011. *Financial Times [CC BY 2.0, via Wikimedia Commons]*.

Page 119: A FARMER TELLING HIS FAMILY, A DOCTOR, A VICAR AND A LAWYER HIS LAST WILL AND TESTAMENT. H.W. Bunbury after G.M. Woodward, Wellcome Images *[CC BY 4.0, via Wikimedia Commons]*.

Page 121: *DOÑA ISABEL LA CATÓLICA DICTANDO SU TESTAMENTO*, detail. Eduardo Rosales *[Public domain, via Wikimedia Commons]*.

Page 124: *A FAMILY GATHERS TO HEAR THE LAST WILL AND TESTAMENT OF A DECEASED MEMBER*. Wellcome Images *[CC BY 4.0, via Wikimedia Commons]*.

Page 125: LE MUSÉE PEGGY GUGGENHEIM (VENISE). 2010. Jean-Pierre Dalbéra, Paris, France *[CC BY 2.0, via Wikimedia Commons]*.

Page 127: CHIHULY AT KEW GARDENS, detail. 2005. Photo by Patche99z *[Public domain, via Wikimedia Commons]*.

Page 129: FIRE HOME. 2007. Durova *[Public domain, via Wikimedia Commons]*.

Page 133: FRUIT ON A TABLE WITH A SMALL DOG. Paul Gauguin. 2014. Photo by Niccolò *[CC BY- SA 3.0 or GFDL, via Wikimedia Commons]*.

Page 135: CARABINIERE A BOLOGNA. 2006. Georges Jansoone *[GFDL, CC-BY-SA-3.0, or CC BY 2.5, via Wikimedia Commons]*.

Page 136: LUXURY GARAGE SALE SIGN. 2013. Pete Unseth *[CC BY-SA 3.0, via Wikimedia Commons]*.

Page 140: SALON DE 1849, AUX TUILERIES. 1849. Theodor Hoffbauer *[Public domain, via Wikimedia Commons]*.

Page 141: CHIPPENDALE SIDE CHAIR, MAKER UNKNOWN, NEW YORK CITY, 1760-1780. 2013. Photo by Daderot *[CC0, via Wikimedia Common]*.

Page 143: ATELIER GIACOMETTI. 2010. Adrian Michael. *[GFDL or CC BY-SA 3.0, via Wikimedia Commons]*.

Page 144: ALBERTO-GIACOMETTI-ETCHING. 2002. Jan Hladík *[CC BY-SA 3.0, via Wikimedia Commons]*.

Page 145: PETER PAN STATUE LONDRES. Photo by Sebjarod *[Public domain, via Wikimedia Commons]*.

Page 146: ENIAC. *[Public domain, via Wikimedia Commons]*.

Page 148: DOLLS OF CLOTH, REINDEER HIDE, MALLARD JAWBONE, AND GLASS BEAD - NENETS PEOPLE, SIBERIA. Museum of Cultures, Helsinki. 2012. Photo by Daderot *[CC0, via Wikimedia Commons]*.

Page 149: LONDON SOTHEBY'S. 2013. Dirk Ingo Franke *[CC BY-SA 3.0, via Wikimedia Commons]*.

Page 151: ELIZABETH TAYLOR, USO, detail. 1986 *[Public domain, via Wikimedia Commons]*.

Page 152: *THE CONNOISSEUR*, detail. Ferdinand Roybet *[Public domain, via Wikimedia Commons]*.

Page 152: LAUGHLIN STEWART'S 1969 CAMARO. John Flandrick *[Used with permission]*.

Page 154: GOODWILL INDUSTRIES THRIFT SHOP-CANTON, MICHIGAN. 2011. Dwight Burdette *[CC BY 3.0, via Wikimedia Commons]*.

Page 156: COMPULSIVE HOARDING APARTMENT. 2009. Grap *[GFDL or CC BY-SA 3.0, via Wikimedia Commons]*.

Page 157: WOMEN SEATED AT OLD SCHOOL DESKS ON THE LAWN TAKE A BREAK DURING AN AUCTION BY EATING PIE SERVED BY LADIES OF WHITE CLOUD, KANSAS, 1974. Patricia D. Duncan, U.S. National Archives and Records Administration *[Public domain, via Wikimedia Commons]*.

Page 159: MARBLES MACRO SIDE, detail. 2011. Glenda Green *[CC BY 3.0, via Wikimedia Commons]*.

Page 159: "HOW MARBLES ARE MADE," *New Zealand Tablet*, Volume XXIX, Issue 9, 28 February 1901. National Library of New Zealand. *[Public domain, via http://paperspast.natlib.govt.nz/periodicals/NZT19010228.2.59]*.

Pages 160-161, 164: GOLD WREATH CIRCA 350 AND CIRCA 300 BC, detail. Photo by Marie-Lan Nguyen. *[Copyright Marie-Lan Nguyen/Wikimedia Commons, via Wikimedia Commons]*.

Page 163: CANDLESTICKS, from the collection of Elizabeth Stewart. John Flandrick. *[Used with permission]*.

Page 167: AUTHOR AND HER OFFICE. 2016. Santi Visalli. *[Used with permission]*.

Author's note: *Collect Value Divest* is a book about how to research what you own, and what you own is, in fact, Material Culture. Created objects, the 'furniture' of our lives, tell us about our personal and public value(s). The books below examine the meanings of belongings and their influence upon and within aesthetic theory. What we are attached to is a metaphor for who we are and the culture we belong to. That's why such objects are called "our belongings."

Abt, Theodor. *Introduction to Picture Interpretation: According to C. G. Jung*. Zurich: Living Human Heritage Publications, 2005.

Aristotle. *Poetics*. Mineola, NY: Dover Publications, 1997.

Behrman, S. N. *Duveen: The Story of the Most Spectacular Art Dealer of All Time*. NY: The Little Bookroom, 1952.

Bordo, Susan. *The Flight to Objectivity: Essays on Cartesianism and Culture*. Albany, NY: State U of New York P, 1987.

Braudel, Fernand. *The Structures of Everyday Life: Civilization and Capitalism 15$^{th}$ – 18$^{th}$ Century* Volume 1. Trans. Sian Reynolds. NY: Harper and Row Publishers Inc., 1985.

Busch, Akiko. *Geography of Home: Writing on Where We Live*. NY: Princeton Architectural

Csikszentmihalyi, Mihaly, and Rick E. Robinson. *The Art of Seeing: An Interpretation of the Aesthetic Encounter*. LA: J. Paul Getty Museum Press, 1990.

---. and Eugene Rochberg-Halton. *The Meaning of Things: Domestic Symbols and the Self*. NY: Cambridge UP, 1999.

Doty, William G. *Picturing Cultural Values in Postmodern America*. Tuscaloosa, AL: The U of Alabama P, 1995.

Douglas, Mary and Baron Isherwood. *The World of Goods: Towards an Anthropology of Consumption*. NY: Routledge, 2001.

Elkins, James. *Pictures and Tears*. NY: Routledge Taylor and Frances Group, 2004.

---. *Stories of Art*. New York, New York: Routledge, 2002.

---. *Visual Literacy*. NY: Routledge Taylor and Frances Group, 2008.

---. *What Painting Is*. New York, New York: Routledge, 2000.

---. *Why Art Cannot Be Taught*. Chicago, IL: U of Illinois P, 2001.

Friedlander, Max J. *On Art and Connoisseurship*. Boston, MA: Beacon Press, 1942.

Fromm, Erich. *To Have Or To Be?*. NY: Bantam Books, 1976.

Gombrich, E. H. *Art and Illusion: A Study in the Psychology of Pictorial Representation*. Princeton, NJ: Princeton UP, 1956, 1972.

---. *Meditations on a Hobby Horse and Other Essays on the Theory of Art*. NY: Phaidon Publishers Inc, 1971.

---. *The Sense of Order: A Study in the Psychology of Decorative Art*. London: Phaidon Press Ltd., 1979.

---. *The Story of Art*. Oxford: Phaidon Press, 1972.

Halle, David. *Inside Culture, Art & Class in the American Home*. Chicago: The U of Chicago P, 1993.

Heidegger, Martin. *What Is a Thing?* Trans. W. B. Barton, Jr. and Vera Deutsch. Chicago: Henry Regnery Co., 1967.

Humes, Edward. *Garbology: Our Dirty Love Affair with Trash*. NY: Avery, 2012.

Ivan, Karp, Christine Mullen Kreamer. *Museums and Communities: The Politics of Public Culture*. Ed. Steven D. Lavine. Washington, DC: Smithsonian Institution Press, 1992.

Janson, H. W. *History of Art*. NY: Harry N. Abrams, 1973.

Josipovici, Gabriel. *Touch*. New Haven, CT: Yale UP, 1996.

Kandel, Eric R. *The Age of Insight: The Quest to Understand the Unconscious in Art, Mind, and Brain*. NY: Random House, 2012.

Larousse. *Dictionary of Painters*. NY: Larousse and Co., 1981.

Liberman, Alexander. *The Artist in His Studio*. NY: The Viking Press, Inc., 1960.

Lowe, M. Donal. *Body in Late-Capitalist USA*. Durham, NC: Duke UP, 1995.

Lynes, Russell. *The Tastemakers: Shaping of American Popular Taste*. NY: Dover Publications, Inc., 1980.

Manguel, Alberto. *Reading Pictures: What We Think About When We Look at Art*. NY: Random House Trade Paperbacks, 2002.

Marquis, Alice Goldfarb. *Art Czar: The Rise and Fall of Clement Greenberg*. Boston, MA: MFA Publications, 2006.

Mason, Christopher. *The Art of the Steal: Inside the Sotheby's-Christie's Auction House Scandal*. NY: Putnam Adult, 2004.

Miller, Daniel. *The Comfort of Things*. Cambridge: Polity Press, 2012.

---. *Consumption and its Consequence*. Cambridge: Polity Press, 2012.

---. *Stuff*. Cambridge: Polity Press, 2010.

---. *Tales from Facebook*. Cambridge: Polity Press, 2011.

--- and Sophie Woodward. *Blue Jeans: The Art of the Ordinary*. Berkley: U of California P, 2012.

Olalquiaga, Celeste. *The Artificial Kingdom: A Treasury of the Kitsch Experience*. NY: Pantheon Books, 1998.

Panmuk, Orhan. *The Innocence of Objects*. Trans. Ekin Oklap. NY: Abrams Publishing, 2012.

Pearce, Susan, M. *On Collecting: An Investigation into Collecting in the European Tradition*. NY: Routledge Taylor and Frances Group, 2005.

Ronald D. Spencer., Ed. *The Expert Versus the Object: Judging Fakes and False Attributions in the Visual Arts*. Oxford, NY: Oxford UP, 2004.

Rueger, Christoph. *Musical Instruments and Their Decoration: Historical Gems of European Culture*. Trans. Peter Underwood. Cincinnati, OH: Seven Hills Books, 1996.

Rybczynski, Witold. *Home: A Short History of an Idea.* NY: Viking Penguin Inc., 1987.

Schapiro, Meyer. *Modern Art, 19th and 20th Centuries.* NY: G. Graziller, 1978.

Schlereth, Thomas, J., Ed, *Material Culture Studies in America.* Walnut Creek, CA: Altamira Press, 1999.

Scholl, Jessie. *Dirty Secret: A Daughter Comes Clean About Her Mother's Compulsive Hoarding.* NY: Gallery Books, 2010.

Secrest, Meryle. *Duveen: A Life in Art.* NY: Alfred A. Knopf, 2004.

Simpson, Colin. *Artful Partners: Bernard Berenson and Joseph Duveen.* NY: MacMillan, 1987.

Thompson, William Irwin. *Coming into Being: Artifacts and Texts in the Evolution of Consciousness.* NY: St. Martin's Press, 1998.

Tilley, Christopher and Webb Keane, Susanne Kuehler, Mike Rowlands and Patricia Spyer. *A Handbook of Material Culture.* London: Sage Publications, 2006.

Tilley, James. *The Language of Ornament.* London: Thomas Hudson, 2001.

Wolfe, Tom. *The Painted Word.* NY: Bantam, 1999.

# INDEX